JESSE MARKEL

ROMEO
AND JULIET

HARBRACE SHAKESPEARE

ROMEO AND JULIET

edited by
Ken Roy

HARCOURT
BRACE
CANADA

Harcourt Brace & Company, Canada
Toronto • Orlando • San Diego • London • Sydney

Harbrace Shakespeare: Series Editor, Ken Roy

Canadian Cataloguing in Publication Data

Shakespeare, William, 1564-1616
    Romeo and Juliet

(Harbrace Shakespeare)
For use in high schools.

I. Roy, Ken.   II. Title.   III. Series

PR2831.A2R69 1987   822.3'3   C87-093766-9

95 96   FP   10 9

Text and cover design: Michael van Elsen Design Inc.
Cover and text illustrations: Laszlo and Marika Gal.
∞ Printed in Canada on acid free paper.

Acknowledgments

The editor and publisher acknowledge the consultants
listed below for their contribution to the development of this
program:

June Bolger
former English Consultant, Secondary Schools, Lakeshore
School Board, Quebec

Robert J. Ireland
Assistant Superintendent of Curriculum (Language Arts),
Metropolitan Toronto Separate School Board

Chris M. Worsnop
Co-ordinator of English, Peel Board of Education, Ontario

To the Reader

You may know something about the play *Romeo and Juliet* already. Perhaps you have older brothers and sisters who have studied the play, or you might have seen the movie. You may have read other kinds of love stories about young people who defied everyone and stubbornly held to their desire to be together. Sometimes these stories ended happily; other times they ended tragically.

Before reading each scene in the play, you will have the opportunity to explore ideas, themes, or personal experiences similar to the ones you will read about. This will help you get ready to read. You might want to discuss your opinions in small groups or, perhaps, write your responses in a journal.

Each scene is also followed by a set of activities related to the issues and problems that arise during the scene. You might want to pause after each scene, or after a group of scenes, or at the end of each act. Whichever you decide, you will see that many of these activities, just like the ones before each scene, call for group work and personal response.

If you would like to use this easy before-and-after framework for getting into the action of the play, discuss with your classmates and your teacher how to set up your journal responses. A date and a heading often will help you to focus and keep track of your own developing feelings.

Now that you have some idea about how the play will be presented in the pages that follow and about the many ways in which you can experience the play, you are probably ready to start your first theme exploration. It is an overview of many of the themes you will meet in the play.

Getting Started

In groups, discuss several of the following questions before you begin reading *Romeo and Juliet*. Record in your journal responses you find particularly interesting or thought-provoking. When you begin reading and discussing the play, you may want to refer to these notes and alter or expand them.

Everyone is familiar with the typical love story in which two young people fall in love and become oblivious to the rest of the world. The young couple are so drawn together that they are willing to go to any lengths for each other, at any cost, regardless of obstacles. There are *always* obstacles, of course. There may be parental disapproval, problems resulting from strained relationships and previous loyalties, and any number of jealousies and hatreds. These obstacles constantly threaten to ruin the relationship before it really has a chance to grow. To the young lovers, these obstacles are merely annoyances encountered on their way to happiness. They are determined that all of their problems can and will be overcome simply because their love is more important than life itself.

1. What stories, plays, or TV shows have you seen in which a young couple in love were determined to have their happiness? How did they turn out? Compare two that you remember. Describe some of the features you think were either similar or different.

2. Most people think that it's necessary for us to control our emotions if society is to be reasonable and safe. However, there are times when people act emotionally. What are some of the feelings that cause people to:
   • fight with each other?
   • defend a friend no matter what?
   • fall in love with each other?
   • fear or resist authority?
   • harm themselves or others?
   • decide it is better to avoid a confrontation than encourage one?
   • decide not to "take the law into their own hands," even though they believe they have been wronged?

3. Can a person really decide that he or she is going to fall in love with another person? Think about this question. If you are familiar with horoscopes, comment on why some people might like to read them.

4. When you have an argument with somebody, how do you attempt to resolve it?

5. When an adult tells you, "I don't think you should do that," how do you usually respond?

6. Sometimes there is a fine line between deciding "Yes, I will" and "No, I will not." Explain how you decide between the two.

The ideas that you have been discussing such as love, hate, friendship, emotion, and reason, are all important *themes* in the play *Romeo and Juliet*. The notes that you have recorded in your journal should help you understand the play as you experience it. Refer to them as you continue your reading.

Dramatis Personae
(Characters in the Play)

Escalus, Prince of Verona
Paris, a young nobleman, relative of the Prince
Montague ⎱ heads of two warring houses
Capulet ⎰
An old man, member of the Capulet family
Romeo, son to Montague
Mercutio, relative of the Prince, friend of Romeo
Benvolio, nephew of Montague, friend of Romeo
Tybalt, nephew of Lady Capulet
Friar Laurence, a Franciscan
Friar John, another Franciscan
Balthasar, servant of Romeo
Sampson ⎱ servants of Capulet
Gregory ⎰
Peter, servant of Juliet's nurse
Abraham, servant of Montague
An Apothecary
Three Musicians
Page to Paris; another Page; an Officer
Lady Montague, wife of Montague
Lady Capulet, wife of Capulet
Juliet, daughter of Capulet
Nurse to Juliet
Citizens of Verona; several men and women, relatives of both
        houses; Maskers, Guards, Watchmen, and Attendants
Chorus
Scene: Verona; Mantua

The Prologue

You might know something about prologues already.
A prologue is a speech that is given before the play
begins. The purpose is to give the audience a preview
of the major events and themes. You may have
noticed this technique being used at the beginning of
some television programs.

In the prologue for *Romeo and Juliet* you are given
the themes and the plot of the play. Two prominent
families (the Capulets and the Montagues) living in
Verona, Italy, are enemies. Their ancient feud
interferes with the love for each other of their children,
the two "star-cross'd lovers," Romeo and Juliet. The
lovers are forced to desperate actions that doom
them to death before the family hatred is finally
resolved.

1   *both . . . dignity:* both equal in status and honour

3   *mutiny:* violence

4   *Where . . . unclean:* Where every citizen (the entire community) is guilty of the blood shed during the fights between members of the community.

5   *fatal:* a pun – both in the grip of death and in the grip of fate

6   *star cross'd:* fated to disaster, to end

7-8   *Whose . . . strife:* whose pitiful and unfortunate death finally brings their parents' feud to an end

9   *fearful . . . love:* the terrifying, predestined course of their love that ends in death; perhaps a nautical metaphor, a mark being a point of navigational reference, therefore suggesting a journey motif in the lives of Romeo and Juliet

11   *but:* except for

12   *two hours' traffic:* the normal time for the performance of an Elizabethan play, which ran from beginning to end without interruption of any kind

14   *What here shall miss:* what is missing in this summary or, perhaps, what you (the audience) have missed here; *toil:* acting, the actors' "work" throughout the remainder of the play in order to communicate the events outlined in the prologue to the viewing audience

Prologue

Enter Chorus.

Two households, both alike in dignity,
  In fair Verona, where we lay our scene,
From ancient grudge break to new mutiny,
  Where civil blood makes civil hands unclean.
From forth the fatal loins of these two foes   5
  A pair of star-cross'd lovers take their life;
Whose misadventured piteous overthrows
  Doth with their death bury their parents' strife.
The fearful passage of their death-mark'd love,
  And the continuance of their parents' rage,   10
Which, but their children's end, nought could remove,
  Is now the two hours' traffic of our stage;
The which if you with patient ears attend,
What here shall miss, our toil shall strive to mend.

                                                 [*Exit.*]

Act 1, Scene 1

In this scene . . .

Unlike the first chapter in a book, where you can go back and check details you missed, the first scene of a play in a theatre or on TV has to make an immediate impact on the audience. It has to get the audience's interest and give basic information so the play can be understood. Therefore, the setting must be established, the characters introduced, and the major conflicts suggested swiftly and dramatically.

As the scene starts, you are suddenly witness to two high-spirited young men who are carrying on a friendly, joking "war of words" with each other. They are the servants of the Capulets. Soon they are confronted by the servants of their hated enemy, the Montagues. The tone of the joking turns harsh and dangerous. A fight breaks out. The main protagonists of the play appear, and we learn something about their personalities.

The main emphasis in this scene is on fighting and the results of deep-seated hatreds. Even the jokes become cruel. You'll hear how the Prince, who is the law-giver, attempts to deal with the situation. Also, you'll get your first introduction to Romeo.

1-4   *on my word . . . collar:* an obscure series of puns dealing with 1) to carry coals: to do a menial job; to endure insults; 2) colliers: coal sellers, therefore endurers of insults; 3) choler: anger; 4) to draw: to carry; also to draw a sword; and 5) collar: hangman's noose

11   *take the wall:* walk nearest the wall. Since garbage was thrown into the street, the safest place to walk was against the wall. The nobility was afforded the privilege of walking nearest the wall. The implication is that the Montagues will be forced into the sewer.

12-18   *That shows . . . wall:* an obscene series of references to sexual assault on Montague's maids, based on a proverbial saying that the weakest are beaten, i.e., pushed to the wall

21-24   *I will . . . maidenheads:* more sexual punning involving sexual assault on women and male boasts about virility. The suggestion is that male bravery is connected with sexual mastery over women as well as with the ability to fight.

Act 1, Scene 1

Verona. A public place.

*Enter Sampson and Gregory, of
the house of Capulet, with swords
and bucklers.*

Sampson: Gregory, on my word, we'll not carry coals.

Gregory: No, for then we should be colliers.

Sampson: I mean, an we be in choler, we'll draw.

Gregory: Ay, while you live, draw your neck out o' the collar.

Sampson: I strike quickly, being moved.   5

Gregory: But thou art not quickly moved to strike.

Sampson: A dog of the house of Montague moves me.

Gregory: To move is to stir, and to be valiant is to stand;
   therefore, if thou are moved, thou runn'st away.

Sampson: A dog of that house shall move me to stand. I   10
   will take the wall of any man or maid of Montague's.

Gregory: That shows thee a weak slave; for the weakest
   goes to the wall.

Sampson: 'Tis true; and therefore women, being the weaker
   vessels, are ever thrust to the wall: therefore I will   15
   push Montague's men from the wall and thrust his
   maids to the wall.

Gregory: The quarrel is between our masters and us their
   men.

Sampson: 'Tis all one, I will show myself a tyrant: when I   20
   have fought with the men, I will be cruel with the
   maids; I will cut off their heads.

Gregory: The heads of the maids?

Sampson: Ay, the heads of the maids, or their maiden-heads;
   take it in what sense thou wilt.   25

Gregory: They must take it in sense that feel it.

Sampson: Me they shall feel while I am able to stand; and
   'tis known I am a pretty piece of flesh.

36   *marry:* swearing – an expression meaning literally, "By the Virgin Mary," in common usage at the time as a rather mild oath

37   *Let us . . . begin:* Let us have them begin the fight and keep the law on our side in that we can claim self-defence. There was a law in effect against public feuding, and heavy punishment was brought down on the perpetrators.

38-39 *as they list:* as they choose to, as they please

40   *bite my thumb:* a rude gesture which, like most rude gestures, is not translatable

52   *I am for you:* I am ready to quarrel with you.

56   *Say "better":* Gregory has spotted Tybalt, feels braver, and eggs Sampson on. The line is not likely directed at Benvolio.

61   *swashing:* slashing

64   *art thou drawn:* is your sword drawn? *heartless hinds:* likely a pun on deer (hind) without a male leader (hart), but also, cowardly followers

Gregory: 'Tis well thou are not fish; if thou hadst, thou hadst
    been poor John: draw thy tool; here comes two of the   30
    house of Montagues.
    [*Enter Abraham and Balthasar.*]
Sampson: My naked weapon is out. Quarrel, I will back
    thee.
Gregory: How! turn thy back and run?
Sampson: Fear me not.   35
Gregory: No, marry; I fear thee!
Sampson: Let us take the law of our sides; let them begin.
Gregory: I will frown as I pass by, and let them take it as
    they list.
Sampson: Nay, as they dare. I will bite my thumb at them;   40
    which is disgrace to them, if they bear it.
Abraham: Do you bite your thumb at us, sir?
Sampson: I do bite my thumb, sir.
Abraham: Do you bite your thumb at us, sir?
Sampson: [*Aside to Gregory*] Is the law of our side, if I say   45
    ay?
Gregory: No.
Sampson: No, sir, I do not bite my thumb at you, sir; but
    I bite my thumb, sir.
Gregory: Do you quarrel, sir?   50
Abraham: Quarrel, sir? No, sir.
Sampson: But if you do, sir, I am for you. I serve as good
    a man as you.
Abraham: No better.
Sampson: Well, sir.   55
    [*Enter Benvolio.*]
Gregory: [*Aside to Sampson.*] Say "better"; here comes one
    of my master's kinsmen.
Sampson: Yes, better, sir.
Abraham: You lie.
Sampson: Draw, if you be men. Gregory, remember thy   60
    swashing blow.   [*They fight.*]
Benvolio: Part, fools!   [*Beating down their weapons.*]
    Put up your swords; you know not what you do.
    [*Enter Tybalt.*]
Tybalt: What, art thou drawn among these heartless hinds?
    Turn thee, Benvolio, look upon thy death.   65

67   *manage:* use

71   *bills . . . partisans:* weapons: A bill consisted of a wicked blade
        on the end of a long wooden shaft; a partisan was basically
        a spear shaft with an axe-head attached to it.

73   *long sword:* the sword used for active combat

74   *crutch:* The implications are that Capulet is too old for any kind
        of fighting and that his threat is all bravado. More significantly,
        this suggests that he has lost all ability to enforce what he
        decrees.

76   *in spite of me:* literally, to spite me; to defy me; to challenge
        me

80-83   *Profaners . . . veins:* ornate language used in a rather tense
        situation, essentially suggesting that weapons have been used
        (stained) in spilling neighbours' blood

85   *mistemper'd:* ill tempered, furious

87   *bred of an airy word:* caused by an off-hand remark spoken
        without thought of the consequences

90   *Verona's ancient citizens:* likely the forefathers who established
        the city, i.e., its founders who, it is implied, established the city
        on the basis of peaceful co-existence.

91   *grave beseeming ornaments:* the clothes they wore that distin-
        guished them as a civilized and ordered people

93   *Canker'd with peace:* rusted from disuse; a canker is a malignant
        sore that eats the flesh and will not heal

95   *forfeit of the peace:* the penalty for breaking the peace will be
        death

Benvolio: I do but keep the peace. Put up thy sword,
  Or manage it to part these men with me.
Tybalt: What, drawn, and talk of peace! I hate the word
  As I hate hell, all Montagues, and thee.
  Have at thee, coward!   [*They fight.*]   70
  [*Enter several of both houses who join the fray; then enter
      Citizens, and Peace-officers with clubs.*]
First Officer: Clubs, bills, and partisans! Strike! Beat them
      down!
  Down with the Capulets! down with the Montagues!
  [*Enter old Capulet in his gown, and Lady Capulet.*]
Capulet: What noise is this? Give me my long sword, ho!
Lady Capulet: A crutch, a crutch! why call you for a
      sword?
Capulet: My sword, I say! Old Montague is come,   75
  And flourishes his blade in spite of me.
  [*Enter old Montague and Lady Montague.*]
Montague: Thou villain Capulet,—Hold me not, let me go.
Lady Montague: Thou shalt not stir a foot to seek a foe.
  [*Enter Prince Escalus with his train.*]
Prince: Rebellious subjects, enemies of peace,
  Profaners of this neighbour-stained steel,—   80
  Will they not hear?—What, ho! you men, you beasts,
  That quench the fire of your pernicious rage
  With purple fountains issuing from your veins,
  On pain of torture, from those bloody hands
  Throw your mistemper'd weapons to the ground,   85
  And hear the sentence of your moved prince.
  Three civil brawls, bred of an airy word,
  By thee, old Capulet and Montague,
  Have thrice disturb'd the quiet of our streets,
  And made Verona's ancient citizens   90
  Cast by their grave beseeming ornaments,
  To wield old partisans, in hands as old,
  Canker'd with peace, to part your canker'd hate.
  If ever you disturb our streets again
  Your lives shall pay the forfeit of the peace.   95
  For this time, all the rest depart away.
  You, Capulet, shall go along with me;
  And, Montague, come you this afternoon,

100   *old Free-town:* a reference from the poem, *Romeus and Juliet*, by Arthur Brooke (which was one of Shakespeare's sources for the play), giving the name of Capulet's castle: Villa Franca

102   *Who . . . abroach?:* Who opened up this ancient feud again? (To broach is to pierce a cask in order to draw off the liquor.)

112   *on part and part:* some on one side and some on the other

116-52 *Madam, an hour . . . as know:* Benvolio, speaking to Lady Montague, says that he was in the same frame of mind as Romeo and that he also wished to keep to himself. Because Romeo is sad, he has been avoiding Benvolio. Benvolio has been avoiding Romeo for the same reasons. Montague confirms that his son is sad, and says that he does not know the exact cause of this melancholy. He then says he is willing to go to any lengths to determine the cause of his son's gloomy state of mind.

116   *worshipp'd:* welcomed

118   *drave:* drove

120   *westward rooteth . . . side:* grows on the west side of the city

122   *made:* went; *ware of me:* aware of my approach

124   *affections:* feelings

125   *busied . . . alone:* absorbed in a problem and wishing to be alone to work it out

126   *humour:* inclination or desire, in this case to be alone

127   *shunn'd:* avoided

131   *all so soon as:* just as soon as

132   *Should:* would

133   *Aurora:* the goddess of the dawn

134   *heavy:* heavy in spirit

135   *pens himself:* shuts himself in

To know our further pleasure in this case,
To old Free-town, our common judgment-place. 100
Once more, on pain of death, all men depart.
[*Exeunt all but Montague, Lady Montague, and Benvolio.*]
Montague: Who set this ancient quarrel new abroach?
Speak, nephew, were you by when it began?
Benvolio: Here were the servants of your adversary
And yours close fighting ere I did approach. 105
I drew to part them. In the instant came
The fiery Tybalt, with his sword prepared,
Which, as he breathed defiance to my ears,
He swung about his head and cut the winds,
Who, nothing hurt withal, hiss'd him in scorn. 110
While we were interchanging thrusts and blows,
Came more and more and fought on part and part,
Till the Prince came, who parted either part.
Lady Montague: O, where is Romeo? Saw you him 'today?
Right glad I am he was not at this fray. 115
Benvolio: Madam, an hour before the worshipp'd sun
Peer'd forth the golden window of the east,
A troubled mind drave me to walk abroad;
Where, underneath the grove of sycamore
That westward rooteth from the city's side, 120
So early walking did I see your son.
Towards him I made, but he was ware of me
And stole into the covert of the wood.
I, measuring his affections by my own,
That most are busied when they're most alone, 125
Pursued my humour, not pursuing his,
And gladly shunn'd who gladly fled from me.
Montague: Many a morning hath he there been seen.
With tears augmenting the fresh morning's dew,
Adding to clouds more clouds with his deep sighs; 130
But all so soon as the all-cheering sun
Should in the farthest east begin to draw
The shady curtains from Aurora's bed,
Away from light steals home my heavy son,
And private in his chamber pens himself, 135
Shuts up his windows, locks fair daylight out,
And makes himself an artificial night.

138   *portentous:* foreboding; *humour:* mood

139   *counsel:* the advice of his friends

142   *importuned:* urged him to tell you

144   *his own affections' counsellor:* taking advice about his feelings from no one

147   *sounding and discovery:* being measured and understood

148   *envious:* malignant

154   *grievance:* cause of grief

155-56 *I would . . . shrift:* I hope you are lucky enough to get from him a true confession of the cause of his grief.

157   *Is . . . young?:* The time drags by for Romeo so slowly that he cannot believe it is still morning

158   *new:* just now

166   *in his view:* when looked at from the point of view of an outsider

167   *in proof:* in actual experience

168   *whose view . . . still:* who is always blind. (Cupid, the god of love in mythology, is usually portrayed as a blind boy with wings who carries a bow and arrows. He shoots at human beings who, as soon as they are wounded by an arrow, fall passionately in love.)

169   *see . . . will:* make us do as he wishes

173   *O brawling love! O loving hate!:* the "hate" is the hatred between the Capulets and the Montagues; the love is Romeo's love which we learn later is for Rosaline, a Capulet. This speech uses a series of oxymorons (figures of speech which link contradictory terms.)

Black and portentous must this humour prove
Unless good counsel may the cause remove.
Benvolio: My noble uncle, do you know the cause? 140
Montague: I neither know it nor can learn of him.
Benvolio: Have you importuned him by any means?
Montague: Both by myself and many other friends;
But he, his own affections' counsellor,
Is to himself—I will not say how true— 145
But to himself so secret and so close,
So far from sounding and discovery,
As is the bud bit with an envious worm
Ere he can spread his sweet leaves to the air
Or dedicate his beauty to the sun. 150
Could we but learn from whence his sorrows grow,
We would as willingly give cure as know.
[*Enter Romeo.*]
Benvolio: See, where he comes! So please you, step aside;
I'll know his grievance, or be much denied.
Montague: I would thou wert so happy by thy stay 155
To hear true shrift. Come, madam, let's away.
                              [*Exeunt Montague and Lady.*]
Benvolio: Good morrow, cousin.
Romeo: Is the day so young?
Benvolio: But new struck nine.
Romeo: Ay me! sad hours seem long.
Was that my father that went hence so fast?
Benvolio: It was. What sadness lengthens Romeo's hours? 160
Romeo: Not having that which, having, makes them short.
Benvolio: In love?
Romeo: Out—
Benvolio: Of love?
Romeo: Out of her favour, where I am in love. 165
Benvolio: Alas, that love, so gentle in his view,
Should be so tyrannous and rough in proof!
Romeo: Alas, that love, whose view is muffled still,
Should, without eyes, see pathways to his will!
Where shall we dine? O me! What fray was here? 170
Yet tell me not, for I have heard it all.
Here's much to do with hate, but more with love:
Why, then, O brawling love! O loving hate!

174   *of nothing first create:* created out of nothing

176   *Mis-shapen . . . forms!:* ugliness mixed with beauty

179   *This love . . . in this:* I am in love, but I see no evidence of love in this fray.

180   *coz:* cousin; (applied rather casually to any close relative)

181   *At thy good . . . oppression:* at what your good heart is saddened by

182   *love's transgression:* the way in which love can be cruel to people

184   *propagate:* increase; *to have it prest:* to have it combined with

187   *fume:* breath

188   *purged:* purified

190   *madness most discreet:* a madness not perceptively evident or obvious

191   *A choking gall . . . sweet:* bitter enough to choke a person, yet sweet enough to sustain a person

196   *sadness:* seriousness

199-200 *Bid a sick . . . ill!:* said, perhaps, more to himself than to Benvolio

205-211 *She'll not . . . gold:* a series of proofs of his love's chastity

206   *Dian's wit:* the wisdom of Diana, the virgin goddess, who managed to avoid Cupid's arrows

209   *stay the siege . . . terms:* wait and allow herself to be attacked, likely by flowery words and propositions

O anything, of nothing first create!
O heavy lightness! serious vanity!   175
Mis-shapen chaos of well-seeming forms!
Feather of lead, bright smoke, cold fire, sick health!
Still-waking sleep, that is not what it is!
This love feel I, that feel no love in this.
Dost thou not laugh?
Benvolio: No, coz, I rather weep.   180
Romeo: Good heart, at what?
Benvolio: At thy good heart's oppression.
Romeo: Why, such is love's transgression.
Griefs of mine own lie heavy in my breast,
Which thou wilt propagate, to have it prest
With more of thine. This love that thou hast shown   185
Doth add more grief to too much of mine own.
Love is a smoke raised with the fume of sighs;
Being purged, a fire sparkling in lovers' eyes;
Being vex'd, a sea nourish'd with lovers' tears.
What is it else? A madness most discreet,   190
A choking gall, and a preserving sweet.
Farewell, my coz.
Benvolio: Soft! I will go along.
An if you leave me so, you do me wrong.
Romeo: Tut, I have lost myself; I am not here.
This is not Romeo; he's some other where.   195
Benvolio: Tell me in sadness, who is that you love?
Romeo: What, shall I groan and tell thee?
Benvolio: Groan! why, no;
But sadly tell me who.
Romeo: Bid a sick man in sadness make his will;
Ah, word ill urged to one that is so ill!   200
In sadness, cousin, I do love a woman.
Benvolio: I aim'd so near, when I supposed you loved.
Romeo: A right good mark-man! And she's fair I love.
Benvolio: A right fair mark, fair coz, is soonest hit.
Romeo: Well, in that hit you miss. She'll not be hit 205
With Cupid's arrow; she hath Dian's wit;
And, in strong proof of chastity well arm'd,
From love's weak childish bow she lives unharm'd.
She will not stay the siege of loving terms,

210   *Nor bide . . . eyes:* nor put up with looks of love

211   *Nor ope . . . gold:* nor accept such gold as would overpower the resistance of a saint

213   *her store:* the reserve of her beauty, since she will leave no children

215   *in that sparing . . . waste:* By sparing herself from having children she is responsible for great waste, since her beauty will not live on.

216-221 *For beauty . . . tell it now:* These lines indicate for the reader Romeo's love for Rosaline though they are not particularly important except to contrast her with Juliet later in the play.

216   *starved with her severity:* destroyed by her unshakable decision not to marry

217   *Cuts . . . posterity:* prevents the future from gaining the beauty that she should have left to it

218-19 *She is too fair . . . despair:* A person so wise and beautiful as she is should not find happiness by making me totally unhappy by causing me to despair.

222   *Be ruled:* be guided, as in, "Take my advice."

224   *by giving liberty . . . eyes:* by letting your eyes be free to look at other beautiful women

225-26 *Tis the way . . . more:* Were I to examine other beauties, I would only be more curious about my love's exquisite beauty.

235   *I'll pay . . . debt:* I will teach you to forget or else I will die in the attempt.

Nor bide the encounter of assailing eyes, 210
Nor ope her lap to saint-seducing gold.
O, she is rich in beauty, only poor
That, when she dies, with beauty dies her store.
Benvolio: Then she hath sworn that she will still live chaste?
Romeo: She hath, and in that sparing makes huge waste; 215
For beauty starved with her severity
Cuts beauty off from all posterity.
She is too fair, too wise, wisely too fair,
To merit bliss by making me despair.
She hath forsworn to love, and in that vow 220
Do I live dead that live to tell it now.
Benvolio: Be ruled by me, forget to think of her.
Romeo: O, teach me how I should forget to think.
Benvolio: By giving liberty unto thine eyes;
Examine other beauties.
Romeo: 'Tis the way 225
To call hers exquisite, in question more.
These happy masks that kiss fair ladies' brows
Being black put us in mind they hide the fair;
He that is strucken blind cannot forget
The precious treasure of his eyesight lost. 230
Show me a mistress that is passing fair,
What doth her beauty serve, but as a note
Where I may read who pass'd that passing fair?
Farewell: Thou canst not teach me to forget.
Benvolio: I'll pay that doctrine, or else die in debt. 235
                                        [*Exeunt.*]

Act 1, Scene 1: Activities

1. Why do you think Shakespeare describes the plot in the Prologue? If you already know what happens, why should you read the play?

2. How old do you think the participants in the street brawl are? Can you think of a situation in which a similar fight might occur today? If you could give some advice to the Prince concerning his handling of the fight, what would you say to him? Would he listen? Why or why not?

3. What suggests that Romeo is a man looking for someone to love? How would you describe his attitude?

4. As a friend, write a letter to Romeo giving him your opinion of what he's doing.

5. List the main characters introduced so far, and describe the personality of each. If you were in charge of casting for a movie, what people would you choose to play these characters? What notes might you, as a director, make in your journal about the personality trait you wanted each actor to emphasize? The director might underline a particular word that should be emphasized when it is spoken.

6. In groups, choose a section of this scene to paraphrase (to rewrite in your own words). Divide up the lines among the members of your group and rehearse these new speeches aloud. You could present your speeches to your class.

7. There are references to the mythological god and goddess Cupid and Diana in this scene. Find out as much as you can about each of these characters. What significance do they have for Romeo in this scene? Why have mythological characters such as Cupid and Diana remained so popular to readers, viewers, and writers, to the present day?

As you do research, discuss your work with the teacher to make sure you are on the right track. Keep all your notes and rough drafts in a folder.

Present a summary of your findings in an essay, a chart, or an audio-visual form at the end of the time specified for this independent activity.

For the next scene . . .

Under what circumstances would you persuade a friend to do something that might create problems for him or her? If a friend tried to persuade you to do something that might bring trouble, what would you do?

Act 1, Scene 2

In this scene . . .

Paris asks Capulet for permission to marry Juliet.
Capulet is hesitant, and no deal is arranged. Capulet
announces a party. Benvolio and Romeo continue
their discussion about love, and Romeo reads the party
invitation issued by Capulet. Benvolio believes that
the party is an excellent opportunity for Romeo to see
that Rosaline (the woman with whom he fancies himself to be in love) is not the most beautiful woman in
Verona. Romeo agrees to go to the party, even though
a servant warns him of the dangers to a Montague
discovered at a Capulet's party.

1   *bound:* obliged to keep the peace

4   *reckoning:* reputation

6   *my suit:* my petition to marry Juliet

9   *She hath . . . years:* My daughter is not yet fourteen years old.

14   *The earth . . . she:* She is the only one of his children to have survived. (In those days, childbirth was very dangerous for both mother and child; frequently both died.)

15   *hopeful . . . earth:* the only child of his body (earth), and she has hopes to inherit Capulet's estate (earth)

17   *My . . . part:* My wishes depend on her assent or agreement.

18-19   *within . . . voice:* My approval (according voice) will be given where she makes her choice.

20   *old accustom'd:* as has been our custom over time

25   *Earth-treading . . . light:* beautiful women whose radiance will light up the night

27   *well-apparell'd:* April is the month when nature itself is dressed in its best apparel of leaves and flowers. In England, spring usually arrives in April; therefore, April is the month when buds and green leaves and flowers appear.

30   *Inherit:* witness or, perhaps, possess

Scene 2

A street.

Enter Capulet, Paris, and Servant.

Capulet: But Montague is bound as well as I,
  In penalty alike; and 'tis not hard, I think,
  For men as old as we to keep the peace.
Paris: Of honourable reckoning are you both;
  And pity 'tis you lived at odds so long.   5
  But now, my lord, what say you to my suit?
Capulet: But saying o'er what I have said before:
  My child is yet a stranger in the world;
  She hath not seen the change of fourteen years.
  Let two more summers wither in their pride,   10
  Ere we may think her ripe to be a bride.
Paris: Younger than she are happy mothers made.
Capulet: And too soon marr'd are those so early made.
  The earth hath swallow'd all my hopes but she,
  She is the hopeful lady of my earth: 15
  But woo her, gentle Paris, get her heart,
  My will to her consent is but a part;
  An she agree, within her scope of choice
  Lies my consent and fair according voice.
  This night I hold an old accustom'd feast,   20
  Whereto I have invited many a guest,
  Such as I love; and you, among the store
  One more, most welcome, makes my number more.
  At my poor house look to behold this night
  Earth-treading stars that make dark heaven light.   25
  Such comfort as do lusty young men feel
  When well-apparell'd April on the heel
  Of limping winter treads, even such delight
  Among fresh female buds shall you this night
  Inherit at my house; hear all, all see,   30
  And like her most whose merit most shall be:

32-33   *Which on . . . none:* When you have had a good look at other girls, my daughter being one of them, you may not then have such a high opinion (reckoning) of her.

38-44   *Find them . . . writ:* a series of puns on occupations, which confuses trades and their tools. Since the servant cannot read, he must ask Romeo to read the list to him so that he can invite the people on the list, as Capulet demanded.

44   *In good time:* a reference to the fortunate arrival of Romeo and Benvolio, who may help him with his problem

45-50   *Tut . . . die:* Benvolio is still pursuing his argument that Romeo can only forget Rosaline by falling in love with another woman; thus, "some new infection to thy eye." It's interesting to note that the imagery used to describe love is that of disease.

51   *Your . . . for that:* Romeo rejects the advice and says that there is no cure for love. (The plantain leaf was used as a cure for various afflictions, including, love.)

54   *bound . . . is:* The treatment of madmen in Elizabethan times was to be put in a straitjacket.

57   *God gi' god-den:* literally, "God give you a good evening."

66   *Mercutio:* Mercutio is a relative of the Prince and even though he is aligned more with the Montagues than with the Capulets he could be invited to the Capulet party.

Which on more view, of many mine being one,
May stand in number, though in reckoning none.
Come, go with me.   [*To Servant, giving a paper.*]
    Go, sirrah, trudge about
Through fair Verona; find those persons out   35
Whose names are written there, and to them say
My house and welcome on their pleasure stay.
                              [*Exeunt Capulet and Paris.*]
Servant: Find them out whose names are written here!
    It is written, that the shoemaker should meddle with his
        yard and the tailor with his last, the fisher with his   40
        pencil and the painter with his nets; but I am sent to
        find those persons whose names are here writ, and
        can never find what names the writing person hath here
        writ. I must to the learned. In good time.
    [*Enter Benvolio and Romeo.*]
Benvolio: Tut, man, one fire burns out another's burning.   45
    One pain is lessen'd by another's anguish;
    Turn giddy, and be holp by backward turning;
    One desperate grief cures with another's languish.
    Take thou some new infection to thy eye,
    And the rank poison of the old will die.   50
Romeo: Your plaintain-leaf is excellent for that.
Benvolio: For what, I pray thee?
Romeo: For your broken shin.
Benvolio: Why, Romeo, art thou mad?
Romeo: Not mad, but bound more than a madman is;
    Shut up in prison, kept without my food,   55
    Whipp'd and tormented and—God-den, good fellow.
Servant: God gi' god-den. I pray, sir, can you read?
Romeo: Ay, mine own fortune in my misery.
Servant: Perhaps you have learned it without book.
    But, I pray, can you read anything you see?   60
Romeo: Ay, if I know the letters and the language.
Servant: Ye say honestly. Rest you merry!
Romeo: Stay, fellow; I can read.
    [*Reads.*] *"Signior Martino and his wife and daughters; County*
        Anselme and his beauteous sisters; the lady widow of   65
        Vitruvio; Signior Placentio and his lovely nieces; Mercutio
        and his brother Valentine; mine uncle Capulet, his wife,

68 *Rosaline:* the first mention of the name of Romeo's love interest

80 *crush a cup:* a colloquialism, like "crack a bottle"

82 *ancient:* well established, customary

85 *unattainted:* unprejudiced, impartial

87 *swan . . . crow:* Swans were symbols of beauty; crows, of ugliness.

88-89 *When . . . fires:* conventional imagery of Courtly Love – "When my eyes, which are religious (their faith is in Rosaline), believe such lies (that other women are as beautiful as Rosaline), may my tears turn into fires."

and daughters; my fair niece Rosaline; Livia; Signior
Valentio and his cousin Tybalt; Lucio and the lovely
Helena."   70

A fair assembly: whither should they come?

Servant: Up.

Romeo: Whither?

Servant: To supper; to our house.

Romeo: Whose house?   75

Servant: My master's.

Romeo: Indeed, I should have ask'd you that before.

Servant: Now I'll tell you without asking: my master is the
great rich Capulet; and if you be not of the house of
Montagues, I pray, come and crush a cup of wine.   80
Rest you merry!   [*Exit.*]

Benvolio: At this same ancient feast of Capulet's
Sups the fair Rosaline whom thou so lovest,
With all the admired beauties of Verona.
Go thither; and, with unattainted eye,   85
Compare her face with some that I shall show,
And I will make thee think thy swan a crow.

Romeo: When the devout religion of mine eye
Maintains such falsehood, then turn tears to fires;
And these, who, often drown'd, could never die,   90
Transparent heretics, be burnt for liars!
One fairer than my love! The all-seeing sun
Ne'er saw her match since first the world begun.

Benvolio: Tut, you saw her fair, none else being by,
Herself poised with herself in either eye;   95
But in that crystal scales let there be weigh'd
Your lady's love against some other maid
That I will show you shining at this feast,
And she shall scant show well that now shows best.

Romeo: I'll go along no such sight to be shown,   100
But to rejoice in splendour of mine own.   [*Exeunt.*]

Act 1, Scene 2: Activities

1. Capulet seems to share a modern view that young marriages, made too hastily, often end in disaster. What, exactly, does he say about the subject? Write a personal journal entry in which you give your views about teenage marriages.

2. Prepare a short dialogue between Capulet and Paris on the subject of marriage that might precede this scene. You will have to decide the following:
   - What approach would Paris use to convince Capulet that he would be an acceptable partner for Juliet?
   - How would Capulet determine whether or not Paris's intentions were genuine and honourable?

   When you create your dialogue, keep the following in mind:
   - It must conform with the main idea (theme) of the scene.
   - It must lead into the conversation within the scene.
   - It must be "in character."
   - It must not change the action of the scene.

   Act out your dialogue for the rest of the class.

3. What can you tell about Paris so far? In your role as casting director, whom would you choose to play the part of Paris?

4. Where is the element of chance (fate, destiny) introduced in this scene?

5. In Scene 1 (line 222) Benvolio says, "Be ruled by me." If you were Romeo, would you be ruled by this man? What do you think is the real purpose of Benvolio's conversation with Romeo?

6. An image is a physical likeness or representation of a person or thing. Lilacs may suggest spring to you and all

that spring as a season means. For someone else, lilacs may not have any special meaning. When people use images in their speech, they are trying to create a feeling or mood. What images does Romeo use in the first two scenes? What mood does he create? Do the images that Romeo uses have associations for you?

7. Discuss with your group the things that you think a playwright should do to capture the attention of an audience at the beginning of a play. Has Shakespeare done any of these things so far? Make a list, and as you continue reading the play, check to see if Shakespeare fulfills your expectations.

For the next scene . . .

What would you do if your parents told you that they had set up a date for you? Have your parents ever discussed marriage with you? Have they ever discussed the responsibilities of marriage and of having children? If so, how have you responded to their comments?

Act 1, Scene 3

In this scene . . .

In this scene we meet Lady Capulet, the Nurse, and Juliet. The Nurse appears as a warm, though somewhat bawdy (obscene) character, who likes to use unusual expressions and suggestive language. However, her affection for Juliet seems genuine enough, as we can see in the exchanges that occur between the two. During the conversation, Lady Capulet attempts to convince Juliet that marriage and child-rearing are a woman's responsibilities – even when that woman is only thirteen or fourteen years old. Juliet is not impressed by her mother's persuasions, despite Lady Capulet's insistence that Paris would make an excellent husband. The conversation is ended by the announcement that the party is starting.

2   *by . . . old:* The Nurse swears by the fact that she was a virgin when she was twelve years old.

3   *ladybird:* a term used for ladies of dubious morality which prompts the next expression, "God forbid" (that she should ever be one of those). To the nurse, of course, the form is a slang term of endearment, the implication being that the Nurse and Juliet are quite close and quite fond of each other.

11   *pretty age:* very attractive and appealing; thus, ready for marriage

14   *teen:* sadness

16   *Lammas-tide:* August 1; Juliet will be fourteen on July 31.

19   *Susan:* the Nurse's daughter. She probably died as a baby, making it possible for the Nurse to have been Juliet's wet nurse, i.e., to have breast-fed her.

20   *Were of an age:* were of the same age

23   *marry:* by the Virgin Mary (a mild oath in those times)

24   *the earthquake:* perhaps an earthquake that occurred in England about 1580

27   *wormwood:* a plant applied to the nipple of a feeding mother to discourage the child from breast-feeding. Wormwood is very bitter.

Scene 3

A room in Capulet's house.

Enter Lady Capulet and Nurse.

Lady Capulet: Nurse, where's my daughter? Call her forth
    to me.
Nurse: Now, by my maidenhead at twelve year old,
    I bade her come. What, lamb! What, ladybird!
    God forbid!—Where's this girl? What, Juliet!
    [*Enter Juliet.*]
Juliet: How now! Who calls?   5
Nurse: Your mother.
Juliet: Madam, I am here. What is your will?
Lady Capulet: This is the matter. Nurse, give leave a while,
    We must talk in secret:—nurse, come back again;
    I have remember'd me, thou's hear our counsel.   10
    Thou know'st my daughter's of a pretty age.
Nurse: Faith, I can tell her age unto an hour.
Lady Capulet: She's not fourteen.
Nurse: I'll lay fourteen of my teeth,—
    And yet, to my teen be it spoken, I have but four,—
    She is not fourteen. How long is it now   15
    To Lammas-tide?
Lady Capulet: A fortnight and odd days.
Nurse: Even or odd, of all days in the year,
    Come Lammas-eve at night shall she be fourteen.
    Susan and she—God rest all Christian souls!—
    Were of an age: well, Susan is with God;   20
    She was too good for me. But, as I said,
    On Lammas-eve at night shall she be fourteen;
    That shall she, marry; I remember it well.
    'Tis since the earthquake now eleven years;
    And she was wean'd,—I never shall forget it—   25
    Of all the days of the year, upon that day.
    For I had then laid wormwood to my dug,
    Sitting in the sun under the dove-house wall;

29   *Mantua:* a summer residence about thirty-two kilometres (twenty miles) from Verona

30   *bear a brain:* have a good memory

34-35 *'twas . . . trudge:* When the dovecote (a pen for doves) shook, she knew it was time to flee, and since then eleven years have passed.

37   *rood:* cross

44   *holidame:* a saint (a personal saint adopted by the Nurse as a protector) on whom she could and did swear for help and protection, and, as in this instance, as a verification of truth

49   *stinted:* stopped

54   *stone:* testicle

60   *God . . . grace:* May God have you as one of His saved or His select.

66   *disposition:* wish or desire or inclination

My lord and you were then at Mantua;—
Nay, I do bear a brain;—but, as I said,   30
When it did taste the wormwood on the nipple
Of my dug and felt it bitter, pretty fool,
To see it tetchy and fall out with the dug!
"Shake", quoth the dove-house; 'twas no need, I trow,
To bid me trudge.   35
And since that time it is eleven years;
For then she could stand alone; nay, by the rood,
She could have run and waddled all about;
For even the day before, she broke her brow.
And then my husband—God be with his Soul!   40
A' was a merry man—took up the child,—
"Yea," quoth he, "dost thou fall upon thy face?
Thou wilt fall backward when thou hast more wit;
Wilt thou not, Jule?" and, by my holidame,
The pretty wench left crying, and said "Ay."   45
To see now how a jest shall come about!
I warrant, an I should live a thousand years,
I never should forget it: "Wilt thou not, Jule?" quoth he;
And, pretty fool, it stinted, and said "Ay."
Lady Capulet: Enough of this; I pray thee, hold thy peace.   50
Nurse: Yes, madam: yet I cannot choose but laugh,
To think it should leave crying, and say "Ay";
And yet, I warrant, it had upon its brow
A bump as big as a young cockerel's stone;
A perilous knock; and it cried bitterly: 55
"Yea," quoth my husband, "fall'st upon thy face?
Thou wilt fall backward, when thou comest to age;
Wilt thou not, Jule?" It stinted and said "Ay."
Juliet: And stint thou too, I pray thee, nurse, say I.
Nurse: Peace, I have done. God mark thee to his grace!   60
Thou wast the prettiest babe that e'er I nursed.
An I might live to see thee married once,
I have my wish.
Lady Capulet: Marry, that "marry" is the very theme
I came to talk of. Tell me, daughter Juliet,   65
How stands your disposition to be married?
Juliet: It is an honour that I dream not of.
Nurse: An honour! were not I thine only nurse,

72   *By my count:* as I remember it

77   *a man of wax:* the perfect figure of a man as a sculptor might model from wax before he cast the figure in bronze as his permanent work of art. The emphasis here is on "wax," which suggests something about the character of Paris, perhaps.

83   *And . . . pen:* and find in his looks a source of delight

85-95 *And see . . . less:* roughly, consult the book of perfect lovers to see how well he conforms to all of its dictates. He is, for one thing, a perfect physical specimen; but that is not his only, or even his best, attribute. The most beautiful fish in the sea may hide their most beautiful aspects within, and frequently men do the same. They keep the best of themselves inside, like a book that is beautiful on the outside but is even more beautiful when it is opened.

       The argument is that if Juliet should marry Paris, she would unlock all the secrets of Paris's golden book.

98   *I'll . . . move:* I will look at him with the intention of liking him, if looking at him is enough to make me like him.

99-100 *But no . . . fly:* I will not go any farther than you allow me to go.

102   *the Nurse cursed:* she is not helping

103   *in extremity:* in confusion

105   *the County stays:* Count Paris is waiting for you.

I would say thou hadst suck'd wisdom from thy teat.
Lady Capulet: Well, think of marriage now; younger than
    you,   70
    Here in Verona, ladies of esteem,
    Are made already mothers. By my count,
    I was your mother much upon these years
    That you are now a maid. Thus then in brief:
    The valiant Paris seeks you for his love.   75
Nurse: A man, young lady! Lady, such a man
    As all the world—why, he's a man of wax.
Lady Capulet: Verona's summer hath not such a flower.
Nurse: Nay, he's a flower; in faith, a very flower.
Lady Capulet: What say you? Can you love the gentleman?   80
    This night you shall behold him at our feast:
    Read o'er the volume of young Paris' face
    And find delight writ there with beauty's pen;
    Examine every married lineament
    And see how one another lends content,   85
    And what obscured in this fair volume lies
    Find written in the margent of his eyes.
    This precious book of love, this unbound lover,
    To beautify him, only lacks a cover.
    The fish lives in the sea, and 'tis much pride   90
    For fair without the fair within to hide.
    That book in many's eyes doth share the glory,
    That in gold clasps locks in the golden story;
    So shall you share all that he doth possess,
    By having him, making yourself no less.   95
Nurse: No less! nay, bigger: women grow by men.
Lady Capulet: Speak briefly, can you like of Paris' love?
Juliet: I'll look to like, if looking liking move;
    But no more deep will I endart mine eye
    Than your consent gives strength to make it fly.   100
    [*Enter Servant.*]
Servant: Madam, the guests are come, supper served up,
    you called, my young lady asked for, the nurse cursed
    in the pantry, and everything in extremity. I must
    hence to wait; I beseech you, follow straight.   [*Exit.*]
Lady Capulet: We follow thee. Juliet, the County stays.   105
Nurse: Go, girl, seek happy nights to happy days. [*Exeunt.*]

Act 1, Scene 3: Activities

1. Three very important characters have been introduced in this scene. From what you've heard so far, how would you describe the personality of each? Whom would you cast for these parts?

2. How would you direct the Nurse on stage – as a sour person who has had an unhappy life or as a jovial, jolly busybody? Perhaps you know someone who has a similar job. What lines in the play would you want an actress playing the part to emphasize?

3. There is much discussion in this scene about marriage. What are the pro-marriage arguments, and how does Juliet respond to them? How would you respond?

4. What is your impression of Juliet after reading this scene?

5. What is the significance of Juliet's response to her mother's question, "Can you like of Paris' love?" (line 97).

6. Now that you've met Juliet, do you think she and Romeo will make a good pair? How do their attitudes about love compare?

7. In groups discuss the following questions:
   - To what extent do you believe that Juliet is capable of making mature decisions about love and marriage at this point in the play?
   - Is Juliet's response to her mother consistent with responses teenage girls might make today?
   - Who do you think should make the final decision about the person you will marry? You might have a debate on marriage.

For the next scene . . .

Think of a situation in which someone persuaded you to do something that you felt wouldn't work out, but you did it anyway. What were the results? If you want to persuade people to do something you think is really important, but they don't really want to do it, what arguments do you use to convince them that they should?

Act 1, Scene 4

In this scene . . .

This scene begins with Romeo and his friends about to attend the Capulet party. The party is an elaborate masque (a spectacle in which a procession of highly costumed and masked people parade through the streets at night carrying torches and accompanied by music). The masked procession arrives at the house where the party is to be held, and a great ball follows.

People who sponsored masques had to be very wealthy because the masques were very costly. Hosts spent large sums of money on decorations, musicians, dancers, actors, and on staging effects.

When we meet Romeo and his friends in this scene, they are costumed and masked and are approaching the gates of the Capulet household. Forms and faces are half-lit by torches, candles, lanterns, and lamps; everything is back-cast by shadows and darkness. Romeo, however, is depressed and not in the mood for a party. In fact, he states that he is so oppressed by love that his soul feels as heavy as lead. Romeo and his friend Mercutio argue about the quality of love. They allude to Cupid, who, traditionally, carries the person struck by his arrow into ecstasies of rapture. Romeo feels that Cupid's arrows bring no such rapture. In fact, he feels as if he has lead weights tied to his feet and his heart.

Mercutio attempts to convince Romeo that he must rise above his depression and lead the party in merriment as he has always done before. He argues that unless Romeo is an enthusiastic participant the Montague group will have a dull time. Romeo agrees to continue with the party. However, he senses something foreboding about the evening. He is very unhappy and feels that his life will be forever shaped by the events of this night.

1-2   *What . . . apology?:* Shall we make a speech excusing ourselves (for having arrived without an invitation) or shall we go in without any apology?

3   *The date . . . prolixity:* Such long-windedness (prolixity) is old-fashioned.

4   *hoodwink'd:* blindfolded (masked)

6   *crow-keeper:* scarecrow

10   *measure:* musical measure; thus, to "measure them a measure" is to dance one dance

11   *ambling:* literally, moving with the gait of a horse, at an easy pace. Here, the reference is to dancing.

12   *heavy:* sad

21   *pitch:* height

29   *visage:* face

Scene 4

A street.

*Enter Romeo, Mercutio, with five
or six Maskers
and Torch-bearers.*

Romeo: What, shall this speech be spoke for our excuse?
　Or shall we on without apology?
Benvolio: The date is out of such prolixity.
　We'll have no Cupid hoodwink'd with a scarf,
　Bearing a Tartar's painted bow of lath,　　　　　　5
　Scaring the ladies like a crow-keeper;
　Nor no without-book prologue, faintly spoke
　After the prompter, for our entrance;
　But let them measure us by what they will,
　We'll measure them a measure and be gone.　　　　10
Romeo: Give me a torch. I am not for this ambling;
　Being but heavy, I will bear the light.
Mercutio: Nay, gentle Romeo, we must have you dance.
Romeo: Not I, believe me. You have dancing shoes
　With nimble soles; I have a soul of lead　　　　　15
　So stakes me to the ground I cannot move.
Mercutio: You are a lover; borrow Cupid's wings,
　And soar with them above a common bound.
Romeo: I am too sore enpierced with his shaft
　To soar with his light feathers, and so bound　　20
　I cannot bound a pitch above dull woe.
　Under love's heavy burden do I sink.
Mercutio: And, to sink in it, should you burden love;
　Too great oppression for a tender thing.
Romeo: Is love a tender thing? It is too rough,　　　25
　Too rude, too boisterous, and it pricks like thorn.
Mercutio: If love be rough with you, be rough with love;
　Prick love for pricking, and you beat love down.
　Give me a case to put my visage in,
　　　　　　　　　　　[Putting on a mask.]

30   *A visor for a visor:* an ugly mask for an ugly face

32   *beetle-brows:* heavy protruding brows

34   *betake him to his legs:* start dancing

36   *rushes:* grasses, leaves, and herbs used to cover the floor

37   *grandsire phrase:* old saying

38   *candle-holder:* a non-participant

39   *The game . . . done:* likely a reference to gambling. When a player is ahead in the game, it is time to leave. (Proverbial, as in "quit while you're ahead.")

40   *dun's the mouse:* likely, "be as quiet as a mouse" (proverbial), though there are numerous intricate puns on "dun/done," lost on us but not on Shakespeare's audience

41   *mire:* mud; likely a reference to a game in which players lifted a heavy log representing a "dun" (a common name for a horse) trapped in the mud

43   *burn daylight:* waste time

46-47   *judgment . . . wits:* common sense

47   *five wits:* five senses

49   *'tis no wit:* it is not wise or intelligent

53   *Queen Mab:* in English folk tales, queen of the fairies ("mab" in Welsh means child). Here Mab is the midwife to men's fancies, i.e., she delivers men's brains of dreams.

57   *atomies:* very small creatures

59   *spinners' legs:* spiders' legs

A visor for a visor! what care I   30
What curious eye doth quote deformities?
Here are the beetle-brows shall blush for me.
Benvolio: Come, knock and enter; and no sooner in,
   But every man betake him to his legs.
Romeo: A torch for me; let wantons light of heart   35
   Tickle the senseless rushes with their heels,
   For I am proverb'd with a grandsire phrase:
   I'll be a candle-holder, and look on.
   The game was ne'er so fair, and I am done.
Mercutio: Tut, dun's the mouse, the constable's own word. 40
   If thou art dun, we'll draw thee from the mire
   Of this sir-reverence love, wherein thou stick'st
   Up to the ears. Come, we burn daylight, ho!
Romeo: Nay, that's not so.
Mercutio: I mean, sir, in delay
   We waste our lights in vain, like lamps by day.   45
   Take our good meaning, for our judgment sits
   Five times in that ere once in our five wits.
Romeo: And we mean well in going to this mask;
   But 'tis no wit to go.
Mercutio: Why, may one ask?
Romeo: I dream'd a dream to-night.
Mercutio: And so did I.   50
Romeo: Well, what was yours?
Mercutio: That dreamers often lie.
Romeo: In bed asleep, while they do dream things true.
Mercutio: O, then, I see Queen Mab hath been with you.
   She is the fairies' midwife, and she comes
   In shape no bigger than an agate-stone   55
   On the fore-finger of an alderman,
   Drawn with a team of little atomies
   Over men's noses as they lie asleep;
   Her waggon-spokes made of long spinners' legs,
   The cover of the wings of grasshoppers;   60
   Her traces of the smallest spider's web;
   Her collars of the moonshine's watery beams;
   Her whip of cricket's bone; the lash, of film;
   Her waggoner a small grey-coated gnat,
   Not half so big as a round little worm   65

78   *smelling out a suit:* sensing the possibilities of gaining a desired office from the king

79   *tithe-pig:* the pig given to the parson as his tithe – one-tenth of the yearly produce

81   *benefice:* a church appointment for which the parson receives money

84   *ambuscadoes:* ambushes; *Spanish blades:* Spanish swords – swords of especially high quality.

85   *healths five fathom deep:* drinking toasts of enormous size

89   *plats:* braids or knots

90   *bakes . . . hairs:* mats and cakes the tangles in the hair said to be put there by the elves

92   *hag:* an evil fairy

96   *nothing:* things without substance, i.e., nonsense

98   *vain:* empty; *fantasy:* illusion; things that are not really present

Prick'd from the lazy finger of a maid:
Her chariot is an empty hazel-nut
Made by the joiner squirrel, or old grub,
Time out o' mind the fairies' coachmakers.
And in this state she gallops night by night   70
Through lovers' brains, and then they dream of love;
O'er courtiers' knees, that dream on court'sies straight;
O'er lawyers' fingers, who straight dream on fees;
O'er ladies' lips, who straight on kisses dream,
Which oft the angry Mab with blisters plagues,   75
Because their breaths with sweetmeats tainted are.
Sometimes she gallops o'er a courtier's nose,
And then dreams he of smelling out a suit;
And sometime comes she with a tithe-pig's tail
Tickling a parson's nose as a' lies asleep,   80
Then dreams he of another benefice;
Sometimes she driveth o'er a soldier's neck,
And then dreams he of cutting foreign throats,
Of breaches, ambuscadoes, Spanish blades,
Of healths five fathom deep; and then anon   85
Drums in his ear, at which he starts and wakes,
And being thus frighted swears a prayer or two
And sleeps again. This is that very Mab
That plats the manes of horses in the night,
And bakes the elf-locks in foul sluttish hairs,   90
Which, once untangled, much misfortune bodes.
This is the hag when maids lie on their backs,
That presses them and learns them first to bear,
Making them women of good carriage:
This is she—
Romeo: Peace, peace, Mercutio, peace!   95
Thou talk'st of nothing.
Mercutio: True, I talk of dreams,
    Which are the children of an idle brain,
    Begot of nothing but vain fantasy,
    Which is as thin of substance as the air
    And more inconstant than the wind, who wooes   100
    Even now the frozen bosom of the north,
    And, being anger'd, puffs away from thence,
    Turning his face to the dew-dropping south.

106   *misgives:* anticipates

107   *consequence:* future occurrence; *yet hanging in the stars:* not yet revealed by the stars (an astrological reference). The suggestion is that human destiny is linked with the workings of the stars and the planets.

108   *begin his fearful date:* begin the inevitable or fateful encounter

109-10   *expire . . . life:* bring my life to its determined end

111   *By some . . . death:* by some useless and meaningless death, coming prematurely

112   *He:* God or Fate (here personified). My life is in the hands of God, or Fate, who determines its course.

113   *lusty:* healthy and strong; full of vitality

Benvolio: This wind you talk of blows us from ourselves;
    Supper is done, and we shall come too late.   105
Romeo: I fear, too early; for my mind misgives
    Some consequence, yet hanging in the stars,
    Shall bitterly begin his fearful date
    With this night's revels, and expire the term
    Of a despised life closed in my breast   110
    By some vile forfeit of untimely death.
    But He that hath the steerage of my course
    Direct my sail! On, lusty gentlemen!
Benvolio: Strike, drum.   *[Exeunt.]*

Act 1, Scene 4: Activities

1. Disguise is important in this scene. Of what use is it, according to Mercutio? Do you agree with him?

2. Most fairy tales suggest that love will triumph in the end and that everyone in the story will live happily ever after. How does Mercutio's Queen Mab speech differ from the usual fairy tale format? Is his speech a warning to Romeo? Write a modern version of Mercutio's speech in which you include his lines, "I talk of dreams,/Which are the children of an idle brain,/Begot of nothing but vain fantasy."

3. If you were a character in this scene, what advice would you give Romeo? What would you say to Mercutio? Develop several lines of dialogue directed at both Romeo and Mercutio which express your views. Where would you fit this dialogue into the play?

4. Why do you think that Romeo and Mercutio are friends? Consider the following:
   • What interests do they have in common?
   • What personality traits do they share?
   • How do they act toward each other?
   • How well do they understand each other's moods?
   • What does each admire about the other?

5. Whom would you prefer as a friend – Romeo or Mercutio? Give reasons to support your choice. Write a journal entry on what you consider to be the most important qualities of friendship.

6. Organize a modern masque. In your planning, consider the following:
   • What is your theme?
   • What will your invitation look like?
   • How will you have your guests dress?
   • What sort of music will you play?

- What kind of food will you serve?
- What other preparations will you make?

You might wish to perform the masque on a "Drama Day."

For the next scene . . .

How many movies and television shows can you name in which the central issue is "love at first sight?" Why are such shows so popular? How often does love at first sight happen in real life?

Act 1, Scene 5

In this scene . . .

This scene occurs in the Capulet home. Capulet welcomes the guests to his masque and invites them all to join in the dance and enjoy themselves. As Capulet and a friend discuss the last time they participated in a masque, Romeo enters. He sees Juliet and marvels at her beauty. Unfortunately, Tybalt recognizes Romeo's voice and knows that he is a Montague. He points him out to Capulet and threatens to kill Romeo. Capulet, however, orders Tybalt not to disturb the feast. Tybalt doesn't agree to anything, but he does leave the party. Romeo and Juliet meet, and they proclaim their love for each other.

2   *trencher:* wooden platter

6   *joint-stools:* small stools made by a joiner (a carpenter)

6-7   *court-cupboard:* a cabinet without doors or drawers used to display; *plate:* the silver dishes and cutlery

8   *marchpane:* marzipan – a paste of ground almonds, sugar, and other sweeteners, often made up into small cakes

13   *great chamber:* the hall of Capulet's house

15-16 *the longer . . . all:* a proverbial saying, probably meaning, "He who lives longest will be the happiest or get the most out of life."

18   *bout:* round of dancing

20   *makes dainty:* pretends to be shy by making excuses

21   *Am I come . . . now?:* "Have I come close to the truth?" or, perhaps, "Do you understand my meaning?"

23   *worn a visor:* worn a mask and danced

27   *A hall, a hall!:* Clear the hall for dancing.

Scene 5

A hall in Capulet's house.

*Musicians waiting. Enter Serving-
men, with napkins.*

First Servant: Where's Potpan, that he helps not to take
away? He shift a trencher! He scrape a trencher!
Second Servant: When good manners shall lie all in one or
two men's hands, and they unwashed too, 'tis a foul
thing.   5
First Servant: Away with the joint-stools, remove the court-
cupboard, look to the plate. Good thou, save me a
piece of marchpane; and, as thou lovest me, let the
porter let in Susan Grindstone and Nell. Antony and
Potpan!   10
Second Servant: Ay, boy, ready.
First Servant: You are looked for and called for, asked for
and sought for, in the great chamber.
Second Servant: We cannot be here and there too.
Cheerly, boys; be brisk a while, and the longer liver take   15
all.   [*They retire behind.*]
[*Enter Capulet, with Juliet and others of his house, meeting
the Guests and Maskers.*]
Capulet: Welcome, gentlemen! Ladies that have their toes
Unplagued with corns will have a bout with you.
Ah, ha! my mistresses, which of you all
Will now deny to dance? She that makes dainty,   20
She, I'll swear, hath corns. Am I come near ye now?
Welcome, gentlemen! I have seen the day
That I have worn a visor and could tell
A whispering tale in a fair lady's ear,
Such as would please; 'tis gone, 'tis gone, 'tis gone.   25
You are welcome, gentlemen! Come, musicians, play.
A hall, a hall! give room! and foot it, girls.
                                   [*Music plays, and they dance.*]

34   *By'r lady:* by the Virgin Mary, a mild oath

37   *Come Pentecost:* come the fiftieth day after Passover, usually the seventh Sunday after Easter (also called Whit Sunday or Whitsuntide)

40   *Will you . . . that?:* I find that hard to believe! (Perhaps colloquially, "You don't mean to tell me!")

41   *ward:* a minor, under the age of twenty-one, still under the responsibility and care of a guardian

42   *doth enrich:* adorns, in the sense of "makes beautiful"

44   *O, she . . . bright!:* Her beauty surpasses the light of the torches.

47   *Beauty too . . . dear!:* beauty too precious for this common world

48   *trooping with crows:* walking with crows; a figure used to convey the contrast between black and white, beauty and ugliness

52   *Forswear:* deny

56   *an antic face:* a grotesque mask

57   *fleer:* sneer; *solemnity:* here meaning festivity or party

58   *by the stock . . . kin:* by the honour of my ancestors

More light, you knaves; and turn the tables up,
And quench the fire, the room is grown too hot.
Ah, sirrah, this unlook'd-for sport comes well.   30
Nay, sit, nay, sit, good cousin Capulet,
For you and I are past our dancing days.
How long is't now since last yourself and I
Were in a mask?
Second Capulet: By'r lady, thirty years.
Capulet: What, man! 'tis not so much, 'tis not so much.   35
   'Tis since the nuptial of Lucentio,
   Come Pentecost as quickly as it will,
   Some five and twenty years; and then we mask'd.
Second Capulet: 'Tis more, 'tis more. His son is elder, sir;
   His son is thirty.
Capulet: Will you tell me that?   40
   His son was but a ward two years ago.
Romeo: [*To a Serving-man.*] What lady is that which doth
      enrich the hand
   Of yonder knight?
Servant: I know not, sir.
Romeo: O, she doth teach the torches to burn bright!
   It seems she hangs upon the cheek of night   45
   Like a rich jewel in an Ethiop's ear;
   Beauty too rich for use, for earth too dear!
   So shows a snowy dove trooping with crows,
   As yonder lady o'er her fellows shows.
   The measure done, I'll watch her place of stand,   50
   And, touching hers, make blessed my rude hand.
   Did my heart love till now? Forswear it, sight!
   For I ne'er saw true beauty till this night.
Tybalt: This, by his voice, should be a Montague.
   Fetch me my rapier, boy. What dares the slave   55
   Come hither, cover'd with an antic face,
   To fleer and scorn at our solemnity?
   Now, by the stock and honour of my kin,
   To strike him dead I hold it not a sin.
Capulet: Why, how now, kinsman! wherefore storm you
      so?   60
Tybalt: Uncle, this is a Montague, our foe;
   A villain that is hither come in spite

66   *bears him . . . gentleman:* carries himself like a dignified gentleman

68   *well-govern'd:* well-behaved

70   *do him disparagement:* treat him in a manner unsuited to his rank

73   *a fair presence:* an agreeable (friendly) manner

74   *ill-beseeming semblance:* unsuitable appearance

77   *goodman boy:* literally, neither a gentleman nor an adult. Tybalt is acting childishly.

77   *go to!:* You will upset everything, so do as I bid. "Go to" means "enough" and is used to express annoyance here.

81   *set cock-a-hoop:* get everything all stirred-up

83   *saucy:* insolent

84   *This trick . . . scathe you:* This behaviour may cause you harm eventually.

85   *contrary:* cross or defy

86   *princox:* insolent young man

89-90   *Patience . . . greeting:* My uncle's patience clashes with my own anger.

91-92   *this intrusion . . . gall:* Romeo's intrusion, which he is now enjoying, will end in bitterness.

93-106 *If I . . . I take:* a sonnet shared by Romeo and Juliet to illustrate the closeness that each feels for the other as soon as they meet

94   *fine:* penalty

To scorn at our solemnity this night.
Capulet: Young Romeo is it?
Tybalt: 'Tis he, that villain Romeo.
Capulet: Content thee, gentle coz, let him alone,   65
   He bears him like a portly gentleman;
   And, to say truth, Verona brags of him
   To be a virtuous and well-govern'd youth.
   I would not for the wealth of all this town
   Here in my house do him disparagement;   70
   Therefore be patient, take no note of him:
   It is my will, the which if thou respect,
   Show a fair presence and put off these frowns,
   An ill-beseeming semblance for a feast.
Tybalt: It fits, when such a villain is a guest.   75
   I'll not endure him.
Capulet: He shall be endured.
  What, goodman boy! I say, he shall; go to!
  Am I the master here, or you? Go to!
  You'll not endure him! God shall mend my soul!
  You'll make a mutiny among my guests!   80
  You will set cock-a-hoop! You'll be the man!
Tybalt: Why, uncle, 'tis a shame.
Capulet: Go to, go to;
  You are a saucy boy. Is 't so, indeed?
  This trick may chance to scathe you; I know what.
  You must contrary me! Marry, 'tis time.—   85
  Well said, my hearts!—You are a princox; go;
  Be quiet, or—More light, more light!—For shame!
  I'll make you quiet.—What, cheerly, my hearts!
Tybalt: Patience perforce with wilful choler meeting
   Makes my flesh tremble in their different greeting.   90
   I will withdraw; but this intrusion shall
   Now seeming sweet convert to bitter gall.   [*Exit.*]
Romeo: [*To Juliet.*] If I profane with my unworthiest hand
   This holy shrine, the gentle fine is this:
  My lips, two blushing pilgrims, ready stand   95
   To smooth that rough touch with a tender kiss.
Juliet: Good pilgrim, you do wrong your hand too much,
   Which mannerly devotion shows in this;
   For saints have hands that pilgrims' hands do touch,

103   *what hands do:* that is, touch

104   *grant thou . . . despair:* Grant what my lips pray for or my faith will turn to despair.

110   *kiss by the book:* can be read either as "You kiss expertly," as in "You studied it in a book," or, "You kiss expertly, but without passion." If the latter, it would be said teasingly.

116   *lay hold of her:* win her to marriage

117   *the chinks:* plenty of gold (because Juliet is the only child of the wealthy Capulet)

118   *my life . . . debt:* My life is at the mercy of my enemy (since I cannot live without Juliet).

120   *the more is my unrest:* The greater is my worry because things can only become worse.

122   *trifling . . . towards:* a simple banquet of light refreshments that will be arriving soon

126   *fay:* faith; *waxes:* grows. Presumably the banquet is ready even as Capulet announces it, thus his line, "Is it e'en so?" At this point he retires and leaves the party.

And palm to palm is holy palmers' kiss.   100
Romeo: Have not saints lips, and holy palmers too?
Juliet: Ay, pilgrim, lips that they must use in prayer.
Romeo: O, then, dear saint, let lips do what hands do;
    They pray, grant thou, lest faith turn to despair.
Juliet: Saints do not move, though grant for prayers' sake.   105
Romeo: Then move not, while my prayer's effect I take.
    Thus from my lips, by thine, my sin is purged.
                                [Kissing her.]
Juliet: Then have my lips the sin that they have took.
Romeo: Sin from my lips? O trespass sweetly urged!
    Give me my sin again.
Juliet: You kiss by the book.   110
Nurse: Madam, your mother craves a word with you.
Romeo: What is her mother?
Nurse: Marry, bachelor,
    Her mother is the lady of the house,
    And a good lady, and a wise and virtuous.
    I nursed her daughter, that you talk'd withal;   115
    I tell you, he that can lay hold of her
    Shall have the chinks.
Romeo: Is she a Capulet?
    O dear account! my life is my foe's debt.
Benvolio: Away, be gone; the sport is at the best.
Romeo: Ay, so I fear; the more is my unrest.   120
Capulet: Nay, gentlemen, prepare not to be gone;
    We have a trifling foolish banquet towards.
    Is it e'en so? Why, then, I thank you all;
    I thank you, honest gentlemen; good-night.
    More torches here! Come on then, let's to bed.   125
    Ah, sirrah, by my fay, it waxes late;
    I'll to my rest.
         [All but Juliet and Nurse begin to go out.]
Juliet: Come hither, nurse. What is yond gentleman?
Nurse: The son and heir of old Tiberio.
Juliet: What's he that now is going out of door?   130
Nurse: Marry, that, I think, be young Petruchio.
Juliet: What's he that follows there, that would not dance?
Nurse: I know not.
Juliet: Go, ask his name.—If he be married,

135   *My grave . . . bed:* These lines are full of ironies. Juliet states she will die if she cannot marry Romeo and, though she does not know it, she will die even if she does. The lines read literally, "My husband will be Death." Death is mentioned many times in the play as Juliet's ultimate lover.

138   *My only love . . . hate!:* To think that the only one I have ever loved is one I should hate.

139   *Too early . . . too late!:* I saw him before I knew who he really was.

140   *Prodigious:* ominous (and therefore likely to lead to terrible misfortune)

My grave is like to be my wedding-bed.   135
Nurse: His name is Romeo, and a Montague,
   The only son of your great enemy.
Juliet: My only love sprung from my only hate!
   Too early seen unknown, and known too late!
   Prodigious birth of love it is to me   140
   That I must love a loathed enemy.
Nurse: What's this? what's this?
Juliet: A rhyme I learn'd even now
   Of one I danced withal.   [*One calls within "Juliet."*]
Nurse: Anon, anon!
   Come, let's away; the strangers all are gone.
                               [*Exeunt.*]

Act 1, Scene 5: Activities

1. Romeo and his friends have no business being at the Capulet party. How, then, do you account for Capulet's conversation with Tybalt? What do you think of Capulet during the course of this scene?

2. What sort of man is Tybalt? Write a page of dialogue between Tybalt and one of his friends that could take place after Tybalt leaves the Capulet party. What will he say? What kind of attitude will he express? Whom would you cast as Tybalt?

3. Knowing what you do about Romeo and Juliet, how do you account for them falling in love so quickly? How much of a role does physical attraction play?

4. Start keeping the diary that either Romeo or Juliet might have kept from the time they met. Keep adding entries as the play progresses.

5. Write a newspaper account of the Capulet ball as it might appear in a morning paper.

6. The Capulet mansion is up for sale. Write a real-estate advertisement that features it as a "hot property."

7. Choose a partner and imagine that you are minor characters at the Capulet ball. Create a conversation between you that will comment on such topics as the following:
   • the general action of the scene
   • the behaviour of specific characters
   • the possible consequences of the actions of the main actors.

   When you "write yourself into the play," be careful not to destroy the overall mood or theme. Act out your dialogue for the rest of the class or for other groups in the class.

Act 1: Consider the Whole Act

1. Write a paper in which you respond to the following questions and statements:
   - What have I discovered so far?
   - What do I want to know more about?
   - What confuses me the most is . . .
   - My impression of . . . is . . .
   - I like/dislike scene . . . because . . .

   You may wish to discuss your responses with others in your group and to add group responses to your own observations.

2. Prepare a list of about five questions you would like to ask a character in this act. Phrase the questions so that they will force the character to reveal as much of his or her personality and character as possible. Conduct an interview in your group, having one person be the character and another person use your questions as the basis for the interview. The questions should be directed at the person who is playing the character. Time your interviews so that they are no longer than five minutes. The success of each interview will be based on the quality of the answers that the questions draw from the character.

3. *Staging a party*
   Act out the sequence at the beginning of Act I, Scene 5 in which we find Capulet having a wonderful time at his own party, welcoming all his guests and enjoying the pageantry of the evening. To help establish the mood of the party, use some of the following ideas:
   - Create some interesting masks for your actors (use the assistance of the art department).
   - Create the impression of wealth with a few well-chosen props.
   - Have a group of musicians provide appropriate music (the music department could assist here).
   - Create the sense of fun and festivity with a minimum of costuming.

- Involve everyone in your class in the party and imagine that you are at a great ball.
- Have a narrator introduce and close the sequence.

Enjoy yourselves!

This activity will require planning and preparation, just like any successful party. Plan well in advance and make your party a memorable one for everybody involved. You might present it to the whole school for an assembly.

4. *Imagine you are an actor*
   Select an emotionally charged speech of about ten lines, such as Romeo's in Scene 1 (lines 183-192) or in Scene 5 (lines 44-53). Practise reading the speech so you can make a presentation to a member of your group or to the class as a whole. Consider the following when preparing your delivery:
   - Vary your pitch and volume.
   - Use pause for effect.
   - Make body language work for you.
   - Breathe as naturally as you can.

   After you have delivered your speech, discuss with your group or the class what your strong points were and how you could improve your presentation.

5. *Make a video*
   This activity is best accomplished in pairs or small groups. Select a part of a scene and decide who will deliver which lines. Rehearse the segment several times and make certain that you are clear about the meaning of the words and lines, the interpretation of the segment, the movement of the characters, and the interactions taking place. Will your group use any costumes or props?

   Before you shoot this segment,
   - Consider the kind of camera shot that you want to use for each frame of your segment: close-up, medium close-up, or distanced.
   - Write a description of exactly what it is that you are going to shoot in precise shooting frames (try not to select

a segment from the scene that is too complicated or that contains too many frames).
- Decide what the audio portion, other than dialogue, will be.
- Think about the beginning and ending of your segment – do they have dramatic impact?

Practise with the camera to get a "feel" for it before you start shooting the segment. Share your video with the rest of the class.

For the next scene

You probably have friends who have demonstrated some pretty strange behaviour when they have fallen in love. Perhaps you have acted strangely when you have been in love. What do you think happens to people when they fall in love? Do you believe that love can be as painful or as wonderful as many popular songs suggest? Explain your answer.

Act 2, Scene 1

In this scene . . .

Benvolio and Mercutio try to find Romeo, but Romeo wants to be alone and hides. Mercutio makes fun of Romeo and the whole idea of romantic love. He indicates that his preference is for physical love. Believing that Romeo will not be found, the two friends decide to go home.

This act begins with a speech by the Chorus. The speech is a summary of what happened in Act 1 and a preview of events about to happen.

1   *old desire:* Romeo's love for Rosaline

2   *young affection:* his new love for Juliet; *gapes:* is eager

6   *Alike:* both lovers

7   *foe supposed:* As a Capulet, Juliet should be regarded as an enemy; *complain:* utter his complaints, laments of love

8   *steal:* get by stealth; *fearful:* dangerous

10   *use:* are accustomed

13   *time means:* time lends the means

14   *Tempering . . . sweet:* moderating their extreme danger with extreme joy

Act 2

Now old desire doth in his death-bed lie,
  And young affection gapes to be his heir;
That fair for which love groan'd for and would die,
  With tender Juliet match'd, is now not fair.
Now Romeo is beloved and loves again,   5
  Alike bewitched by the charm of looks,
But to his foe supposed he must complain,
  And she steal love's sweet bait from fearful hooks.
Being held a foe, he may not have access
  To breathe such vows as lovers use to swear;   10
And she as much in love, her means much less
  To meet her new-beloved anywhere.
But passion lends them power, time means, to meet,
  Tempering extremities with extreme sweet.   *[Exit.]*

79

1   *go forward:* return home, move away

2   *Turn back . . . centre out:* Romeo's body is the dull earth which
     revolves around Juliet, its centre. The centre of the body to
     which everything was believed to gravitate was the heart, and
     since Romeo's heart is now with Juliet, she is the object to
     which he must gravitate. Juliet is light, but Romeo is "dull" or
     lacking light.

6   *Nay, I'll conjure too:* I shall not just call him, but shall call up
     his spirit with phrases suitable to one in love; that is, I shall use
     magic to make him appear.

7   *humours!:* moods

8   *in the likeness of a sigh:* since lovers are given to sighing

9   *Speak . . . satisfied:* Utter just one lover's rhyme and I shall be
     convinced you are a typical lover and not yourself.

11   *gossip:* friend, one in whom you confide; *Venus:* Cupid's mother,
     goddess of love

13-14 *Young Abraham Cupid . . . beggar maid:* Mercutio compares
       Cupid with "Abraham men" – beggars and thieves who, like
       Cupid, were half-naked.

14   *King Cophetua:* the hero of a popular ballad, who fell in love
     with a humble peasant girl and married her

16   *ape:* fools; apes were trained to mimic humans; *conjure him:*
     raise him up.

18   *high forehead:* a high forehead was a sign of great beauty.
     Portraits of women of this time often show them as having high
     foreheads.

20   *demesnes:* regions or areas (a bawdy reference)

23-29 *This . . . up him:* It would anger him to raise a spirit belonging
       to someone other than himself in his mistress's circle of lovers,
       letting it stand there until she, by her magical powers, satisfied
       it and made it disappear."

27   *some spite:* something done to cause hurt to a person

Scene 1

*A lane by the wall of Capulet's
orchard.*

Enter Romeo.

Romeo: Can I go forward when my heart is here?
  Turn back, dull earth, and find thy centre out.
        [*He climbs the wall, and leaps down within it.*]
  [*Enter Benvolio and Mercutio.*]
Benvolio: Romeo! my cousin Romeo!
Mercutio: He is wise;
  And, on my life, hath stolen him home to bed.
Benvolio: He ran this way, and leap'd this orchard wall.   5
  Call, good Mercutio.
Mercutio: Nay, I'll conjure too.
  Romeo! humours! madman! passion! lover!
  Appear thou in the likeness of a sigh!
  Speak but one rhyme, and I am satisfied;
  Cry but "Ay me!" pronounce but "love" and "dove";   10
  Speak to my gossip Venus one fair word,
  One nick-name for her purblind son and heir,
  Young Abraham Cupid, he that shot so trim,
  When King Cophetua loved the beggar-maid!
  He heareth not, he stirreth not, he moveth not;   15
  The ape is dead, and I must conjure him.
  I conjure thee by Rosaline's bright eyes,
  By her high forehead and her scarlet lip,
  By her fine foot, straight leg and quivering thigh,
  And the demesnes that there adjacent lie,   20
  That in thy likeness thou appear to us!
Benvolio: An if he hear thee, thou wilt anger him.
Mercutio: This cannot anger him: 'twould anger him
  To raise a spirit in his mistress' circle
  Of some strange nature, letting it there stand   25
  Till she had laid it and conjured it down;
  That were some spite: my invocation

31   *To be consorted . . . night:* to keep company with the night, which has the same mood as he has (that is, dark and depressed)

33   *cannot hit the mark:* cannot find the object that it seeks because it cannot see

34   *medlar-tree:* has fruit like a small brown apple that is eaten only when it has decayed or is over-ripe. There is also a pun on the word meddle which has sexual connotations.

38   *An open-arse:* the common name for the fruit of the medlar tree; *poperin:* a type of pear that originated in Poperinghle, Belgium. (This is a corruption of the name of the place of origin.)

39   *I'll to my truckle-bed:* I'll go to my trundle-bed (one on wheels, or a baby bed); that is, "I'm innocent in affairs of this kind."

40   *field-bed:* bed in the open air

Is fair and honest; in his mistress' name
I conjure only but to raise up him.
Benvolio: Come, he hath hid himself among these trees,   30
To be consorted with the humorous night.
Blind is his love and best befits the dark.
Mercutio: If love be blind, love cannot hit the mark.
Now will he sit under the medlar-tree,
And wish his mistress were that kind of fruit   35
As maids call medlars when they laugh alone.
O, Romeo, that she were, O that she were
An open-arse, thou a poperin pear!
Romeo, good-night; I'll to my truckle-bed;
This field-bed is too cold for me to sleep.   40
Come, shall we go?
Benvolio: Go, then; for 'tis in vain
To seek him here that means not to be found.

                              [*Exeunt.*]

Act 2, Scene 1: Activities

1. Mercutio continually ridicules people who are in love. Do you share his views, or do you think that he might be hiding his own feelings about love?

2. Create a portrait of Mercutio. Make your portrait as complete as possible from the information you have so far. You might develop your portrait through a video-taped interview between Mercutio and an interviewer. Plan the interview questions carefully so that you obtain the information you want.

3. Draw a cartoon or a comic strip as Mercutio might draw it showing Romeo hopelessly in love. Write a caption for your cartoon.

4. From the conversations between Benvolio and Mercutio, how do you think the two characters are different from each other?

5. If you were Benvolio, how would you have answered Mercutio's argument about love? As Benvolio, what would you have said to Romeo? Write Benvolio a letter and tell him what he should have done.

For the next scene . . .

How would you handle a situation in which you were forbidden by your family to associate with a young man or woman whom you really wanted to see? Do you believe it's possible for two young people to fall in love when they don't really know very much about each other?

Act 2, Scene 2

In this scene . . .

Romeo visits the Capulet mansion at night. While hiding in the garden, he sees Juliet on a balcony and over-hears her declare that she loves him. Romeo makes his presence known, and the two discuss their love. Juliet agrees to marry Romeo if his intentions are honourable. Romeo assures her that he is indeed honourable. The two part, reluctantly, and Romeo goes off to make the necessary wedding preparations.

1   *He:* Mercutio, whom, it appears, Romeo has overheard. It is easy for Mercutio to laugh at the injuries inflicted by love when he has never been hurt by love himself.

2   *soft!* quiet, be still

4   *envious:* the moon is jealous of Juliet's beauty which is greater than its own

7   *her maid:* virgins were the servants of Diana, goddess of chastity and the moon (itself a symbol of chastity).

8   *vestal:* virgin. Vesta, the goddess of the hearth, was, like Diana, sworn to chastity. *sick;* pale

12   *what of that?:* that doesn't matter.

17   *spheres:* In Elizabethan times it was believed that the planets moved around the earth, which was the centre of the universe, and that each heavenly body (planet or star) moved in its own sphere. The idea here is that if Juliet's eyes replaced two of the stars in the spheres they would light up the entire sky, being brighter than the stars; and if two stars replaced Juliet's eyes, the fairness of her face would make those stars seem dim.

18   *they:* the stars

21   *airy region:* the heavens

28   *a winged messenger of heaven:* an angel

Scene 2

Capulet's orchard.

Enter Romeo.

Romeo: He jests at scars that never felt a wound.

                             [*Juliet appears above at a window.*]

But, soft! what light through yonder window breaks?

It is the east, and Juliet is the sun!

Arise, fair sun, and kill the envious moon,

Who is already sick and pale with grief   5

That thou, her maid, art far more fair than she.

Be not her maid, since she is envious;

Her vestal livery is but sick and green,

And none but fools do wear it; cast it off.

It is my lady, O, it is my love!   10

O, that she knew she were!

She speaks, yet she says nothing; what of that?

Her eye discourses; I will answer it.

I am too bold, 'tis not to me she speaks.

Two of the fairest stars in all the heaven,   15

Having some business, do entreat her eyes

To twinkle in their spheres till they return.

What if her eyes were there, they in her head?

The brightness of her cheek would shame those stars,

As daylight doth a lamp; her eyes in heaven   20

Would through the airy region stream so bright

That birds would sing and think it were not night.

See, how she leans her cheek upon her hand!

O, that I were a glove upon that hand,

That I might touch that cheek!

Juliet: Ay me!

Romeo: She speaks!   25

O, speak again, bright angel! for thou art

As glorious to this night being o'er my head,

As is a winged messenger of heaven

30   *fall back:* are amazed that he can accomplish such a thing

31   *bestrides:* rides, as in riding a horse

32   *sails . . . air:* rides effortlessly without fear of injury

33   *wherefore art thou Romeo?:* Why is your name Romeo (the name of a Montague)?

34   *refuse:* reject

39   *though not a:* even if you were not named

40-44 *What's . . . name:* Juliet questions whether a name "makes" a person.

46   *owes:* owns, possesses

47   *doff:* put aside

48   *for thy name:* in exchange for your name

53   *stumblest:* comes unexpectedly; *counsel:* secret thoughts; confession

61   *dislike:* displease

66-69 *With . . . me:* a practised response, typical of a courtly lover. Though Romeo may believe he means it, he has no experience with love, and so he mouths the words that should be felt. The irony is that, in his mouthing of the words, he is really expressing his true feelings, but he is doing so in the idiom of the courtly love convention. There is little genuine passion here.

Unto the white-upturned wondering eyes
Of mortals that fall back to gaze on him   30
When he bestrides the lazy-pacing clouds
And sails upon the bosom of the air.
Juliet: O Romeo, Romeo! wherefore art thou Romeo?
    Deny thy father and refuse thy name;
    Or, if thou wilt not, be but sworn my love,   35
    And I'll no longer be a Capulet.
Romeo: [*Aside.*] Shall I hear more, or shall I speak at this?
Juliet: 'Tis but thy name that is my enemy;
    Thou art thyself, though not a Montague.
    What's Montague? It is nor hand, nor foot,   40
    Nor arm, nor face, nor any other part
    Belonging to a man. O, be some other name!
    What's in a name? That which we call a rose
    By any other name would smell as sweet;
    So Romeo would, were he not Romeo call'd,   45
    Retain that dear perfection which he owes
    Without that title. Romeo, doff thy name,
    And for thy name which is no part of thee
    Take all myself.
Romeo: I take thee at thy word.
    Call me but love, and I'll be new baptized;   50
    Henceforth I never will be Romeo.
Juliet: What man art thou that thus bescreen'd in night
    So stumblest on my counsel?
Romeo: By a name
    I know not how to tell thee who I am.
    My name, dear saint, is hateful to myself,   55
    Because it is an enemy to thee;
    Had I it written, I would tear the word.
Juliet: My ears have yet not drunk a hundred words
    Of that tongue's utterance, yet I know the sound.
    Art thou not Romeo and a Montague?   60
Romeo: Neither, fair maid, if either thee dislike.
Juliet: How camest thou hither, tell me, and wherefore?
    The orchard walls are high and hard to climb,
    And the place death, considering who thou art,
    If any of my kinsmen find thee here.   65
Romeo: With love's light wings did I o'erperch these walls;

67   *stony limits:* stone walls

68   *And . . . attempt:* The more the challenge to love, the more it can accomplish.

73   *I am proof:* I am protected (against their hatred).

78   *prorogued:* postponed (without the fulfillment of our love)

82   *pilot:* person that assists the captain of a ship to navigate treacherous waters that could otherwise wreck the ship

88   *Fain would . . . form:* Gladly would I stick to the conventions.

89   *but farewell compliment!:* but so much for polite behaviour

98   *fond:* much in love

99   *'haviour light:* behaviour too light-hearted, as if I don't really mean it

101   *strange:* reserved

106   *discovered:* revealed to you

For stony limits cannot hold love out,
And what love can do that dares love attempt;
Therefore thy kinsmen are no let to me.
Juliet: If they do see thee, they will murder thee.　　　70
Romeo: Alack, there lies more peril in thine eye
　　Than twenty of their swords! Look thou but sweet,
　　And I am proof against their enmity.
Juliet: I would not for the world they saw thee here.
Romeo: I have night's cloak to hide me from their eyes;　　75
　　And but thou love me, let them find me here.
　　My life were better ended by their hate,
　　Than death prorogued, wanting of thy love.
Juliet: By whose direction found'st thou out this place?
Romeo: By love, that first did prompt me to inquire;　　80
　　He lent me counsel and I lent him eyes.
　　I am no pilot; yet, wert thou as far
　　As that vast shore wash'd with the farthest sea,
　　I would adventure for such merchandise.
Juliet: Thou know'st the mask of night is on my face,　　85
　　Else would a maiden blush bepaint my cheek
　　For that which thou has heard me speak to-night.
　　Fain would I dwell on form, fain, fain deny
　　What I have spoke; but farewell compliment!
　　Dost thou love me? I know thou wilt say "Ay,"　　90
　　And I will take thy word; yet, if thou swear'st,
　　Thou mayst prove false. At lovers' perjuries,
　　They say, Jove laughs. O gentle Romeo,
　　If thou dost love, pronounce it faithfully;
　　Or if thou think'st I am too quickly won,　　95
　　I'll frown and be perverse and say thee nay,
　　So thou wilt woo; but else, not for the world.
　　In truth, fair Montague, I am too fond,
　　And therefore thou mayst think my 'haviour light;
　　But trust me, gentleman, I'll prove more true　　100
　　Than those that have more cunning to be strange.
　　I should have been more strange, I must confess,
　　But that thou overheard'st, ere I was ware,
　　My true love's passion; therefore pardon me,
　　And not impute this yielding to light love,　　105
　　Which the dark night hath so discovered.

110   *circled orb:* circular orbit. The moon was considered to be the symbol of changeableness because of its continuously changing shape.

114   *god of my idolatry:* god whom I worship

116   *joy:* take pleasure

118   *too rash . . . unadvised:* too quick and impulsive and against good judgment

131   *frank:* generous

132   *the thing I have:* my love for you

133   *bounty:* generosity

137   *Anon:* at once

141   *Too . . . substantial:* too beautiful to be real

Romeo: Lady, by yonder blessed moon I swear
    That tips with silver all these fruit-tree tops—
Juliet: O, swear not by the moon, th' inconstant moon,
    That monthly changes in her circled orb,   110
    Lest that thy love prove likewise variable.
Romeo: What shall I swear by?
Juliet: Do not swear at all;
    Or, if thou wilt, swear by thy gracious self,
    Which is the god of my idolatry,
    And I'll believe thee.
Romeo: If my heart's dear love—   115
Juliet: Well, do not swear. Although I joy in thee,
    I have no joy of this contract to-night.
    It is too rash, too unadvised, too sudden,
    Too like the lightning, which doth cease to be
    Ere one can say "it lightens." Sweet, good-night!   120
    This bud of love, by summer's ripening breath,
    May prove a beauteous flower when next we meet.
    Good-night, good-night! as sweet repose and rest
    Come to thy heart as that within my breast!
Romeo: O, wilt thou leave me so unsatisfied?   125
Juliet: What satisfaction canst thou have to-night?
Romeo: The exchange of thy love's faithful vow for mine.
Juliet: I gave thee mine before thou didst request it;
    And yet I would it were to give again.
Romeo: Wouldst thou withdraw it? For what purpose, love?   130
Juliet: But to be frank, and give it thee again.
    And yet I wish but for the thing I have.
    My bounty is as boundless as the sea,
    My love as deep; the more I give to thee,
    The more I have, for both are infinite.   135
                          [*Nurse, calls within.*]
    I hear some noise within; dear love, adieu!
    Anon, good nurse! Sweet Montague, be true.
    Stay but a little, I will come again.   [*Exit, above.*]
Romeo: O blessed, blessed night! I am afeard,
    Being in night, all this is but a dream,   140
    Too flattering-sweet to be substantial.
    [*Re-enter Juliet, above.*]
Juliet: Three words, dear Romeo, and good-night indeed.

143   *bent:* intention

145   *procure:* arrange

146   *rite:* marriage ceremony

155   *want:* be without

159   *tassel-gentle:* male peregrine falcon, the noblest of the falcons; thus, "I wish I had the falconer's control to lure back this noblest of the species."

160   *Bondage . . . aloud:* Because of the dangers, she can speak only in a whisper.

161   *Echo:* in Greek mythology, a nymph who wasted away for her love of Narcissus until nothing was left of her but her voice

If that thy bent of love be honourable,
Thy purpose marriage, send me word to-morrow,
By one that I'll procure to come to thee,   145
Where and what time thou wilt perform the rite;
And all my fortunes at thy foot I'll lay,
And follow thee my lord throughout the world.
Nurse: [*Within.*] Madam!
Juliet: I come, anon.—But if thou mean'st not well,   150
   I do beseech thee—
Nurse: [*Within.*] Madam!
Juliet: By and by, I come:—
   To cease thy suit, and leave me to my grief.
   To-morrow will I send.
Romeo: So thrive my soul—
Juliet: A thousand times good-night!

                                        [*Exit, above.*]

Romeo: A thousand times the worse, to want thy light.   155
   Love goes toward love, as schoolboys from their books,
   But love from love, toward school with heavy looks.

                                        [*Retiring slowly.*]

[*Re-enter Juliet, above.*]
Juliet: Hist! Romeo, hist! O, for a falconer's voice,
   To lure this tassel-gentle back again!
   Bondage is hoarse, and may not speak aloud;   160
   Else would I tear the cave where Echo lies.
   And make her airy tongue more hoarse than mine,
   With repetition of my Romeo's name.
Romeo: It is my soul, that calls upon my name.
   How silver-sweet sound lovers' tongues by night,   165
   Like softest music to attending ears!
Juliet: Romeo!
Romeo: My dear?
Juliet: At what o'clock to-morrow
   Shall I send to thee?
Romeo: At the hour of nine,
Juliet: I will not fail; 'tis twenty years till then.
   I have forgot why I did call thee back.   170
Romeo: Let me stand here till thou remember it.
Juliet: I shall forget, to have thee still stand there,
   Remembering how I love thy company.

177   *wanton's bird:* child's pet bird

179   *gyves:* shackles

187   *so sweet to rest:* having so sweet a resting place

188   *ghostly:* spiritual father, that is, the priest who advises him about spiritual matters

189   *my dear hap:* the good fortune that has happened to me

Romeo: And I'll still stay, to have thee still forget,
    Forgetting any other home but this.   175
Juliet: 'Tis almost morning; I would have thee gone:—
    And yet no further than a wanton's bird;
    Who lets it hop a little from her hand,
    Like a poor prisoner in his twisted gyves,
    And with a silken thread plucks it back again,   180
    So loving-jealous of his liberty.
Romeo: I would I were thy bird.
Juliet: Sweet, so would I;
    Yet I should kill thee with much cherishing.
    Good-night, good-night! Parting is such sweet sorrow
    That I shall say good-night till it be morrow.   185
                            [Exit, above.]
Romeo: Sleep dwell upon thine eyes, peace in thy breast!
    Would I were sleep and peace, so sweet to rest!
    Hence will I to my ghostly father's cell,
    His help to crave, and my dear hap to tell.   *[Exit.]*

Act 2, Scene 2: Activities

1. Soliloquies are speeches in which actors talk to the audience about themselves and their intentions. The other characters in the play are either not present or don't hear what is said. In lines 2-25, Romeo delivers a soliloquy. Is Romeo believable in his soliloquy? Explain your answer. Would you say the same things under the circumstances if you were Romeo? Why or why not?

2. What kinds of statements does Romeo make to Juliet about his love for her? Do you believe that he is sincere? Discuss your response with your group or the whole class.

3. Do you believe that Juliet is sincere in her responses to Romeo, or do you think she is leading him on? In your own words, summarize what Juliet says to Romeo.

4. Do Romeo and Juliet express their feelings for each other as you might under similar circumstances? What similarities and/or differences do you notice? In your journal, write an account of the first time that you fell in love. To what extent did you act and feel like either Romeo or Juliet?

5. Why do you think the word "love" is repeated so many times in this scene?

For the next scene . . .

What advice would you give to a friend who you felt was making a hasty or unwise decision? What is your experience of the kind of advice adults tend to give teenagers about falling in love?

Act 2, Scene 3

In this scene . . .

This scene occurs in the early morning, shortly after Romeo has left Juliet. Romeo goes to meet Friar Laurence, his friend and religious confessor, who advises Romeo to be cautious. Friar Laurence is willing to perform the marriage – he loves Romeo as a son, and he hopes this marriage will end the Montague-Capulet feud. However, he points out that it was not such a long time ago that Romeo was in love with Rosaline and that perhaps Romeo is acting hastily.

3   *flecked:* dappled, covered with spots

4   *Titan:* here, the sun-god who crosses the sky in his chariot, the sun

7   *up-fill this osier cage:* fill this wicker basket

8   *baleful weeds:* ordinarily harmful, but possessing, for those with knowledge, medicinal qualities

11   *divers:* different

14   *None but for some:* All have some (virtues)

15   *mickle:* much, large; *grace:* bounty (i.e., heavenly blessing)

22   *And vice . . . dignified:* And evil may, through the right action, turn into good.

23   *infant:* as yet undeveloped

25-26   *For this . . . heart:* If smelt, it cheers every part of us; if tasted, it stops all the senses by stopping the heart (i.e., it kills us).

27-28   *Two such . . . will:* So in man, as in herbs, two opposing forces, goodness and evil, always exist.

Scene 3

Friar Laurence's cell.

*Enter Friar Laurence, with a
basket.*

Friar Laurence: The grey-eyed morn smiles on the frowning
   night,
Chequering the eastern clouds with streaks of light,
And flecked darkness like a drunkard reels
From forth day's path and Titan's fiery wheels.
Now, ere the sun advance his burning eye,   5
The day to cheer and night's dank dew to dry,
I must up-fill this osier cage of ours
With baleful weeds and precious-juiced flowers.
The earth, that's nature's mother, is her tomb;
What is her burying grave, that is her womb;   10
And from her womb children of divers kind
We sucking on her natural bosom find,
Many for many virtues excellent,
None but for some, and yet all different.
O, mickle is the powerful grace that lies   15
In herbs, plants, stones, and their true qualities;
For nought so vile that on the earth doth live
But to the earth some special good doth give;
Nor aught so good but, strain'd from that fair use,
Revolts from true birth, stumbling on abuse.   20
Virtue itself turns vice, being misapplied;
And vice sometime's by action dignified.
Within the infant rind of this small flower
Poison hath residence and medicine power;
For this, being smelt, with that part cheers each part;   25
Being tasted, slays all senses with the heart.
Two such opposed kings encamp them still
In man as well as herbs, grace and rude will;
And where the worst is predominant,

30 *canker:* canker-worm, larva that feeds on leaves

31 *Benedicite!:* May God bless you.

33 *argues a distemper'd head:* indicates a disturbed state of mind

37 *unbruised:* unhurt, carefree; *unstuff'd:* not filled with troubled thoughts

38 *golden:* rich, healthful

40 *distemperature:* mental upset

51 *both our remedies:* the healing of both of us

52 *physic:* healing power (in this case, the power to marry them)

54 *steads:* helps

55 *homely:* simple or clear; *drift:* meaning

56 *Riddling . . . shrift:* If you confess to me in riddles, I shall absolve you (present absolution, i.e., free you from sin) in an equally obscure manner.

60 *all combined:* completely united

63 *pass:* go along

65 *Saint Francis:* being of the Franciscan Order, the Friar swears by his patron saint

Full soon the canker death eats up that plant.   30
[*Enter Romeo.*]
Romeo: Good morrow, father.
Friar Laurence: Benedicite!
  What early tongue so sweet saluteth me?
  Young son, it argues a distemper'd head
  So soon to bid good morrow to thy bed.
  Care keeps his watch in every old man's eye,   35
  And where care lodges, sleep will never lie;
  But where unbruised youth with unstuff'd brain
  Doth couch his limbs, there golden sleep doth reign;
  Therefore thy earliness doth me assure
  Thou art up-roused with some distemperature;   40
  Or if not so, then here I hit it right,
  Our Romeo hath not been in bed to-night.
Romeo: That last is true; the sweeter rest was mine.
Friar Laurence: God pardon sin! Wast thou with Rosaline?
Romeo: With Rosaline, my ghostly father? No!   45
  I have forgot that name, and that name's woe.
Friar Laurence: That's my good son; but where hast thou
    been, then?
Romeo: I'll tell thee, ere thou ask it me again.
  I have been feasting with mine enemy,
  Where on a sudden one hath wounded me,   50
  That's by me wounded; both our remedies
  Within thy help and holy physic lies.
  I bear no hatred, blessed man, for, lo,
  My intercession likewise steads my foe.
Friar Laurence: Be plain, good son, and homely in thy drift;   55
  Riddling confession finds but riddling shrift.
Romeo: Then plainly know my heart's dear love is set
  On the fair daughter of rich Capulet:
  As mine on hers, so hers is set on mine;
  And all combined, save what thou must combine   60
  By holy marriage. When and where and how
  We met, we woo'd, and made exchange of vow,
  I'll tell thee as we pass; but this I pray,
  That thou consent to marry us to-day.
Friar Laurence: Holy Saint Francis, what a change is here!   65
  Is Rosaline, that thou didst love so dear,

69   *Jesu Maria:* O Jesus, son of Mary

72   *To season . . . taste:* to preserve a love that was not genuine

79   *sentence:* proverb

80   *Women . . . men:* When men are so weak, women may be excused for sinning.

87-88   *O, she knew . . . spell:* She did not return your love, for she knew your protestations of love consisted merely of memorized phrases and were not from the heart. The figure is of a child, who cannot yet spell, pretending to read.

93   *stand on:* depend for my happiness on

So soon forsaken? Young men's love then lies
Not truly in their hearts, but in their eyes.
Jesu Maria, what a deal of brine
Hath wash'd thy sallow cheeks for Rosaline!   70
How much salt water thrown away in waste,
To season love, that of it doth not taste!
The sun not yet thy sighs from heaven clears,
Thy old groans ring yet in mine ancient ears;
Lo, here upon thy cheek the stain doth sit   75
Of an old tear that is not wash'd off yet.
If e'er thou wast thyself and these woes thine,
Thou and these woes were all for Rosaline.
And art thou changed? Pronounce this sentence then:
Women may fall, when there's no strength in men.   80
Romeo: Thou chid'st me oft for loving Rosaline.
Friar Laurence: For doting, not for loving, pupil mine.
Romeo: And bad'st me bury love.
Friar Laurence: Not in a grave,
   To lay one in, another out to have.
Romeo: I pray thee, chide not; she whom I love now   85
   Doth grace for grace and love for love allow;
   The other did not so.
Friar Laurence: O, she knew well
   Thy love did read by rote that could not spell.
   But come, young waverer, come, go with me,
   In one respect I'll thy assistant be;   90
   For this alliance may so happy prove,
   To turn your households' rancour to pure love.
Romeo: O, let us hence; I stand on sudden haste.
Friar Laurence: Wisely and slow; they stumble that run
   fast.   [*Exeunt.*]

Act 2, Scene 3: Activities

1. What is your evaluation of Friar Laurence based on his soliloquy at the beginning of this scene? Whom would you cast as the Friar?

2. You are the director of a production of *Romeo and Juliet.* At what point during Friar Laurence's speech would you have Romeo arrive on stage? Justify your decision on the basis of whether or not you would want Romeo to hear any of Friar Laurence's speech. Decide whether the timing of Romeo's entrance would make any difference to the way in which the scene finally turns out.

3. If you were Ann Landers and overheard the conversation between Friar Laurence and Romeo, what advice would you offer Romeo in your column? Write the column, share it with your group, and find out their reactions.

4. If someone said to you, "I stand on sudden haste" (line 93), what advice might you give to him or her? Compare your advice with that given by Friar Laurence to Romeo. How are they similar and in what ways do they differ? Do you like your own better? Explain your answer.

5. Marriage customs have varied over the centuries. With the help of the librarian, research marriage customs from Roman times to our own. Decide what they have in common and how they differ. Create a topic that could be included in a publication called "Marriage Through the Ages." Decide whether marriage customs have or have not changed significantly over the ages. Consider what kind of marriage ceremony you might choose for yourself. Talk with your teacher to make sure you have a manageable topic. Keep all your notes with your rough drafts in a separate folder. Prepare a written, oral, or visual account of your findings and conclusions when you have completed this project.

For the next scene . . .

Think of an incident in which an adult assisted a teenager
with a plan that the adult had no business assisting in. What
was the result? Why did the adult agree to help?

Act 2, Scene 4

In this scene . . .

Most of this scene is humorous, and we finally see Romeo having fun with everyone. Many of the jokes revolve around the latest craze – rapier fighting – and the rules, regulations, and jargon that accompanied that skill. Much of the jesting is sexual, and the Nurse is a good-natured target for many of the jokes. In this scene, we learn that Mercutio hates Tybalt, and that he has the courage and the physical strength to confront Tybalt, a noted fighter. We also learn some details of the marriage plans. Romeo gives the Nurse instructions that he and Juliet shall be married at Friar Laurence's cell that very afternoon. The Nurse agrees to deliver this information to Juliet.

11   *answer the letter's master:* respond to the challenge by consenting to fight

15   *pin:* centre, the black peg which held the target in place

16   *blind bow-boy:* Cupid; *butt-shaft:* blunt arrow used for target practice at the butts. The butt was the backing for the target.

19   *cats:* "Tybalt" or "Tyb" was a common name for a cat.

20   *captain of compliments:* master of etiquette

20-21   *as . . . prick-song:* strictly according to proper form. Mercutio compares fencing to music. In these lines, Mercutio is mocking the new fashion in duelling which favoured the rapier rather than the sword and which employed great formality. Fighting by the book is not for Mercutio.

22-23   *rests me . . . bosom:* poises his rapier while a musician would count "one, two" and runs you through on the count of "three"; *minim:* the shortest note in music; *rest:* a pause in music; Mercutio means that Tybalt (when he is fighting) makes two movements with his sword, pausing for a brief moment after each thrust, and then pierces to the heart with his third stroke.

23-24   *the very butcher . . . button:* His thrust is so accurate he can strike a button on a doublet.

24-25   *of the very . . . cause:* of the first rank among duellists and one who will fight on the slightest provocation

25   *the first . . . cause:* terms used in the delivery of the challenge to a duel

26   *passado:* a forward step and thrust in fencing; *punto reverso:* back-handed stroke; *hai:* home-thrust, the hit

28-29   *The pox of . . . fantasticoes:* A plague on these fantastic people with their affected duelling jargon; *new tuners of accent:* fellows who try to improve on the language and who sound affected

29-30   *a very good blade:* a very good fencer; *tall:* valiant (here said in mockery of the new duelling etiquette)

Scene 4

A street.

Enter Benvolio and Mercutio.

Mercutio: Where the devil should this Romeo be?
  Came he not home to-night?
Benvolio: Not to his father's; I spoke with his man.
Mercutio: Ah, that same pale hard-hearted wench, that
  Rosaline,
  Torments him so, that he will sure run mad.   5
Benvolio: Tybalt, the kinsman of old Capulet,
  Hath sent a letter to his father's house.
Mercutio: A challenge, on my life.
Benvolio: Romeo will answer it.
Mercutio: Any man that can write may answer a letter.   10
Benvolio: Nay, he will answer the letter's master, how he
  dares, being dared.
Mercutio: Alas, poor Romeo! he is already dead; stabbed
  with a white wench's black eye; shot through the ear
  with a love song; the very pin of his heart cleft with   15
  the blind bow-boy's butt-shaft: and is he a man to
  encounter Tybalt?
Benvolio: Why, what is Tybalt?
Mercutio: More than prince of cats I can tell you. O, he is
  the courageous captain of compliments. He fights as   20
  you sing prick-song; keeps time, distance, and proportion; rests me his minim rest, one, two, and the
  third in your bosom: the very butcher of a silk button, a duellist, a duellist; a gentleman of the very first
  house, of the first and second cause. Ah, the immortal   25
  passado! the *punto reverso!* the *hai!*
Benvolio: The what?
Mercutio: The pox of such antic, lisping, affecting fantasticoes; these new tuners of accent! "By Jesu, a very
  good blade! a very tall man! a very good whore!" Why,   30

31   *grandsire:* grandfather – Mercutio addresses Benvolio as one old-fashioned man to another.

32   *flies:* little fellows buzzing about with their duelling phrases

33   *fashion-mongers:* merchants of smart new phrases; *perdona – mi's:* people who pretend to be fashionable (by using foreign phrases)

35   *bones:* there is a pun on the French "bon"

37   *without his roe:* he is only part of himself

38   *fishified:* made into a fish

38-39   *Now is he . . . flowed in:* Now he will write love-sonnets such as Petrarch (an Italian poet of the 14th century) composed to Laura (the lady he loved). *to his lady:* compared with Romeo's love

40-41   *berhyme her:* write poetry about her

41-42   *Dido . . . Thisbe:* Mercutio names some of the famous women of myth and history; *hildings:* good for nothings

42   *grey-eye:* considered attractive in a woman

43   *Signior . . . bonjour!:* Mercutio makes fun of the fashionable use of foreign words in English as a sign of sophistication.

50   *strain courtesy:* be forgiven for forgetting his manners

52   *bow in the hams:* be very polite, bow to the knees, curtsy (hams = knees)

59   *pump:* shoe; *well-flowered:* dress shoes were punched with holes to form a pattern of flowers

61   *single sole:* pumps were single-soled for dancing

64   *O . . . singleness!:* a bad joke remarkable only in that it's so bad

68   *wild-goose chase:* In a wild goose horse race, the horses set out on even terms, but when one obtained the lead he might take whatsoever wild course he desired and the other had to follow.

is not this a lamentable thing, grandsire, that we
should be thus afflicted with these strange flies, these
fashion-mongers, these *perdonami's*, who stand so
much on the new form, that they cannot sit at ease on
the old bench? O, their bones, their bones!   35
[*Enter Romeo.*]
Benvolio: Here comes Romeo, here comes Romeo.
Mercutio: Without his roe, like a dried herring: O flesh,
flesh, how art thou fishified! Now is he for the numbers
that Petrarch flowed in. Laura to his lady was but a
kitchen-wench; marry, she had a better love to berhyme   40
her; Dido, a dowdy; Cleopatra, a gipsy; Helen and
Hero, hildings and harlots; Thisbe, a grey eye or so,
but not to the purpose. Signior Romeo, *bonjour*! There's
a French salutation to your French slop. You gave
us the counterfeit fairly last night.   45
Romeo: Good morrow to you both. What counterfeit did I
give you?
Mercutio: The slip, sir, the slip; can you not conceive?
Romeo: Pardon, good Mercutio, my business was great, and
in such a case as mine a man may strain courtesy.   50
Mercutio: That's as much as to say, such a case as yours
constrains a man to bow in the hams.
Romeo: Meaning, to curtsy.
Mercutio: Thou hast most kindly hit it.
Romeo: A most courteous exposition.   55
Mercutio: Nay, I am the very pink of courtesy.
Romeo: Pink for flower.
Mercutio: Right.
Romeo: Why, then is my pump well flowered.
Mercutio: Well said! Follow me this jest now till thou hast   60
worn out thy pump, that, when the single sole of it
is worn, the jest may remain, after the wearing, solely
singular.
Romeo: O single-soled jest, solely singular for the singleness!
Mercutio: Come between us, good Benvolio; my wits faint.   65
Romeo: Switch and spurs, switch and spurs; or I'll cry a
match.
Mercutio: Nay, if thy wits run the wild-goose chase, I have
done; for thou hast more of the wild-goose in one of

71 *for the goose:* as a fool

76 *sweeting:* a sweet apple used for making sauce served with roast goose

79 *cheveril:* kid skin, which is pliable. Mercutio is saying, "You can make your little wit go a long way."

80 *ell:* forty-five inches (about 114 cm)

86 *natural:* fool

87 *bauble:* the fool's stick carried by a professional jester

89-90 *against the hair:* against the grain (here, against my will)

95 *goodly gear:* fine business

96 *A sail:* The nurse apparently looks like a ship under full sail. Mercutio refers to her size as well as her appearance.

97 *a shirt and a smock:* a metonymy for a man and a woman. Metonymy (meta = as, onoma = name) is a figure of speech which substitutes an attribute of a thing for the thing itself, for example, "crown" for "king," "turf" for "horse-racing," "grid-iron" for "football field," "the diamond" for "baseball infield," "a shirt and a smock" for "a man and a woman"

100 *My fan:* The fans of the time were often so large they had to be carried by servants.

104 *God ye good den:* May God give you good evening (referring to any-time after noon).

105 *Is it good den?:* Is it so late as afternoon?

107 *dial:* sun dial or clock; *prick:* point

thy wits than, I am sure, I have in my whole five.   70
Was I with you there for the goose?
Romeo: Thou wast never with me for anything when thou
    wast not there for the goose.
Mercutio: I will bite thee by the ear for that jest.
Romeo: Nay, good goose, bite not.   75
Mercutio: Thy wit is a very bitter sweeting; it is a most sharp
    sauce.
Romeo: And is it not well served in to a sweet goose?
Mercutio: O, here's a wit of cheveril, that stretches from an
    inch narrow to an ell broad!   80
Romeo: I stretch it out for that word "broad"; which added
    to the goose, proves thee far and wide a broad goose.
Mercutio: Why, is not this better now than groaning for
    love? Now art thou sociable, now art thou Romeo, now
    art thou what thou art, by art as well as by nature: for   85
    this drivelling love is like a great natural, that runs
    lolling up and down to hide his bauble in a hole.
Benvolio: Stop there, stop there.
Mercutio: Thou desirest me to stop in my tale against the
    hair.   90
Benvolio: Thou wouldst else have made thy tale large.
Mercutio: O, thou art deceived; I would have made it short:
    for I was come to the whole depth of my tale, and
    meant indeed to occupy the argument no longer.
Romeo: Here's goodly gear.   95
    [*Enter Nurse and Peter.*]
Mercutio: A sail, a sail!
Benvolio: Two, two; a shirt and a smock.
Nurse: Peter!
Peter: Anon!
Nurse: My fan, Peter.   100
Mercutio: Good Peter, to hide her face; for her fan's the
    fairer of the two.
Nurse: God ye good morrow, gentlemen.
Mercutio: God ye good den, fair gentlewoman.
Nurse: Is it good den?   105
Mercutio: 'Tis no less, I tell you; for the bawdy hand of
    the dial is now upon the prick of noon.
Nurse: Out upon you! what a man are you!

110   *mar:* disfigure, ruin

112   *quoth a':* said he

116   *fault:* want

119   *is the worst well?:* Does this "worst," which Romeo applies to himself, satisfy you?

121   *confidence:* conference, the nurse tends to use malapropisms. A malapropism is a misuse of a word that is mistaken for one resembling it. The term is derived from a character, Mrs. Malaprop, who was constantly using such expressions as "illiterate him" for "obliterate him."

122   *indite:* invite; Benvolio makes fun of the nurse's malapropism.

123   *bawd:* a woman who runs a brothel, also a hare; *So ho!:* the cry of the hunter when a hare is sighted

125   *lenten pie:* a meatless pie eaten during Lent (note the pun on hare/hair)

126   *hoar:* old (here it is used as a pun on "whore"); *spent:* used up. The song itself, with its pun, is quite suggestively obscene.

127-132 *An . . . spent:* a bawdy song based on the hare as both animal and "loose woman"

137   *"lady, lady, lady":* Mercutio sings the chorus of a popular ballad of the time.

138   *merchant:* used with contempt

139   *ropery:* roguery (jokes)

143   *And a':* if he

146   *flirt-gills:* flirting gills, women of loose behaviour. (Gill is the feminine of Jack, as in Jack and Jill.)

Romeo: One, gentlewoman, that God hath made for himself
to mar.   110
Nurse: By my troth, it is well said: "for himself to mar,"
quoth a'? Gentlemen, can any of you tell me where I
may find the young Romeo?
Romeo: I can tell you; but young Romeo will be older when
you have found him than he was when you sought   115
him. I am the youngest of that name, for fault of a
worse.
Nurse: You say well.
Mercutio: Yea, is the worst well? Very well took, i' faith;
wisely, wisely.   120
Nurse: If you be he, sir, I desire some confidence with you.
Benvolio: She will indite him to some supper.
Mercutio: A bawd, a bawd, a bawd! So ho!
Romeo: What hast thou found?
Mercutio: No hare, sir; unless a hare, sir, in a lenten pie,   125
that is something stale and hoar ere it be spent.

> *[Sings.]*
>
> An old hare hoar,
> And an old hare hoar,
> Is very good meat in lent;
> But a hare that is hoar,   130
> Is too much for a score,
> When it hoars ere it be spent.

Romeo, will you come to your father's? We'll to dinner
thither.
Romeo: I will follow you.   135
Mercutio: Farewell, ancient lady; farewell,   *[Singing.]*
"lady, lady, lady."   *[Exeunt Mercutio and Benvolio.]*
Nurse: Marry farewell. I pray you, sir, what saucy merchant
was this, that was so full of his ropery?
Romeo: A gentleman, nurse, that loves to hear himself talk, 140
and will speak more in a minute than he will stand to
in a month.
Nurse: An a' speak anything against me, I'll take him down,
an a' were lustier than he is, and twenty such Jacks;
and if I cannot, I'll find those that shall. Scurvy   145
knave! I am none of his flirt-gills; I am none of his

147   *skains-mates:* fighting partners

173   *shrift:* confession

175   *shrived:* be given absolution (necessary before the sacrament of marriage can be received)

181   *tackled stair:* a rope ladder, like the tackle of a ship (as in "block and tackle" – a mechanism of ropes and pulleys used to raise and lower sails)

182   *top-gallant:* the highest point. The top-gallant sail is above (i.e., exceeds the height of) the top-sail.

183   *convoy:* means of access

184   *quit:* reward; *pains:* troubles

skains-mates. [*Turning to Peter.*] And thou must stand
by too, and suffer every knave to use me at his
pleasure?

Peter: I saw no man use you at his pleasure; if I had, my   150
weapon should quickly have been out. I warrant you,
I dare draw as soon as another man, if I see occasion
in a good quarrel, and the law on my side.

Nurse: Now, afore God, I am so vexed, that every part about
me quivers. Scurvy knave! Pray you, sir, a word: and   155
as I told you, my young lady bade me inquire you out;
what she bade me say I will keep to myself. But first
let me tell ye, if ye should lead her into a fool's paradise, as they say, it were a very gross kind of behaviour, as they say; for the gentlewoman is young, and,   160
therefore, if you should deal double with her, truly
it were an ill thing to be offered to any gentlewoman,
and very weak dealing.

Romeo: Nurse, commend me to thy lady and mistress.
I protest unto thee—   165

Nurse: Good heart, and, i' faith, I will tell her as much.
Lord, Lord, she will be a joyful woman.

Romeo: What wilt thou tell her, nurse? Thou dost not mark
me.

Nurse: I will tell her, sir, that you do protest; which, as I   170
take it, is a gentlemanlike offer.

Romeo: Bid her devise
Some means to come to shrift this afternoon;
And there she shall at Friar Laurence' cell
Be shrived and married. Here is for thy pains.   175

Nurse: No, truly, sir; not a penny.

Romeo: Go to; I say you shall.

Nurse: This afternoon, sir? Well, she shall be there.

Romeo: And stay, good nurse;—behind the abbey wall
Within this hour my man shall be with thee,   180
And bring thee cords made like a tackled stair;
Which to the high top-gallant of my joy
Must be my convoy in the secret night.
Farewell; be trusty, and I'll quit thy pains.
Farewell; commend me to thy mistress.   185

Nurse: Now God in heaven bless thee! Hark you, sir.

189   *"Two may . . . away":* Two people can keep a secret, but not three.

193-94 *fain lay knife aboard:* gladly win her. The figure is of soldiers with knives boarding a ship and winning it for themselves as a prize.

196   *properer:* more handsome

197   *clout:* cloth

198   *versal world:* whole world; *rosemary:* the flower of remembrance and weddings

199   *letter:* the same letter

201   *the dog's name:* the letter "R" was called the dog's letter because it sounds like a dog's growling. "Rs" were pronounced much farther back in the throat than they are today and the sound was much more guttural (harsh and throaty).

201-202 *R . . . No:* she was going to say, "R" is for the dog, but stops and says instead that Romeo's name does not begin with a harsh sound.

203   *sententious:* sentence (another malapropism). "Sentence" is used to mean a proverb or clever and amusing saying.

Romeo: What say'st thou, my dear nurse?

Nurse: Is your man secret? Did you ne'er hear say,
  "Two may keep counsel, putting one away"?

Romeo: I warrant thee, my man's as true as steel.   190

Nurse: Well, sir; my mistress is the sweetest lady—Lord,
  Lord! when 'twas a little prating thing,—O, there is a
  nobleman in town, one Paris, that would fain lay knife
  aboard; but she, good soul, had as lief see a toad, a
  very toad, as see him. I anger her sometimes and tell   195
  her that Paris is the properer man; but, I'll warrant
  you, when I say so, she looks as pale as any clout in
  the versal world. Doth not rosemary and Romeo
  begin both with a letter?

Romeo: Ay, nurse; what of that? Both with an R.   200

Nurse: Ah, mocker! that's the dog's name. R is for the—
  No; I know it begins with some other letter—and she
  hath the prettiest sententious of it, of you and rosemary, that it would do you good to hear it.

Romeo: Commend me to thy lady.   205

Nurse: Ay, a thousand times.   [*Exit Romeo.*]
  Peter!

Peter: Anon!

Nurse: Peter, take my fan, and go before and apace.
                              [*Exeunt.*]

Act 2, Scene 4: Activities

1. Which of Tybalt's qualities does Mercutio talk about? How does his description of Tybalt make you feel about Tybalt? Think of somebody that you know or have heard about who resembles Tybalt. How do you feel about the person?

2. In what ways does the conversation between Romeo and Mercutio suggest that they have a very strong friendship? Is there someone with whom you have a similar friendship? If so, what is it about that person that allows you to tease and joke easily together?

3. What do the exchanges between Benvolio, Mercutio, Romeo, and the Nurse add to our understanding of the character of Romeo? What do they tell us about the character of the Nurse?

4. Rewrite the dialogue between the Nurse and Romeo. Compare your version with the original. What did you do that Shakespeare didn't do? Write about the problems you encountered and any thoughts you have about how you may have changed the theme.

5. Do you think that the Nurse is wise to act as an intermediary between Romeo and Juliet? Why do you think she assumes such a role?

6. Why do you think that this scene is in the play at all? Could it possibly be cut? Justify your reasons for either keeping it or cutting it.

For the next scene . . .

In your opinion, is it possible for one person to devote himself or herself totally to another person?

Act 2, Scene 5

In this scene . . .

Juliet has been waiting three hours for the promised word from Romeo. The Nurse arrives back and makes Juliet's anxiety more intense by refusing to answer the direct questions Juliet asks. She finally delivers the message that Juliet is to meet Romeo at Friar Laurence's cell, where the marriage will be performed.

6   *louring:* gloomy

7   *nimble-pinion'd doves:* swift-winged doves which in mythology draw the chariot of Venus

9   *highmost hill:* at the height

12   *affections:* desires; *blood:* passion

14   *bandy her:* send her to and bring her back from. Juliet wishes that the Nurse could be like a tennis ball so that she and Romeo could bandy the Nurse between them.

Scene 5

Capulet's orchard.

Enter Juliet.

Juliet: The clock struck nine when I did send the nurse;
  In half an hour she promised to return.
  Perchance she cannot meet him; that's not so.
  O, she is lame! Love's heralds should be thoughts,
  Which ten times faster glide than the sun's beams   5
  Driving back shadows over louring hills;
  Therefore do nimble-pinion'd doves draw love.
  And therefore hath the wind-swift Cupid wings.
  Now is the sun upon the highmost hill
  Of this day's journey, and from nine till twelve   10
  Is three long hours, yet she is not come.
  Had she affections and warm youthful blood,
  She would be as swift in motion as a ball;
  My words would bandy her to my sweet love,
  And his to me;   15
  But old folks, many feign as they were dead;
  Unwieldy, slow, heavy and pale as lead.
  [*Enter Nurse and Peter.*]
  O God, she comes! O honey nurse, what news?
  Hast thou met with him? Send thy man away.
Nurse: Peter, stay at the gate.   [*Exit Peter.*] 20
Juliet: Now, good sweet nurse,—O Lord, why look'st thou
      sad?
  Though news be sad, yet tell them merrily;
  If good, thou shamest the music of sweet news
  By playing it to me with so sour a face.
Nurse: I am a-weary, give me leave a while.   25
  Fie, how my bones ache! What a jaunt have I had!
Juliet: I would thou hadst my bones, and I thy news.
  Nay, come, I pray thee, speak; good, good nurse speak.

36   *stay the circumstance:* await the details

38   *simple:* foolish

50   *My back . . . side:* the nurse is having Juliet massage her sup-
      posedly aching back

51   *Beshrew:* a mild curse, in the sense of "a plague on"

52   *jaunting:* walking

62   *hot:* eager; *trow:* believe

65   *coil:* fuss, bother

Nurse: Jesu, what haste! Can you not stay a while?
Do you not see that I am out of breath? 30
Juliet: How art thou out of breath, when thou hast breath
To say to me that thou art out of breath?
The excuse that thou dost make in this delay
Is longer than the tale thou dost excuse.
Is thy news good, or bad? Answer to that; 35
Say either, and I'll stay the circumstance.
Let me be satisfied, is't good or bad?
Nurse: Well, you have made a simple choice; you know not
how to choose a man. Romeo! no, not he; though his
face be better than any man's, yet his leg excels all 40
men's; and for a hand, and a foot, and a body,
though they be not to be talk'd on, yet they are past
compare. He is not the flower of courtesy, but, I'll
warrant him, as gentle as a lamb. Go thy ways, wench;
serve God. What, have you dined at home? 45
Juliet: No, no! But all this did I know before.
What says he of our marriage? What of that?
Nurse: Lord, how my head aches! What a head have I!
It beats as it would fall in twenty pieces.
My back o't' other side,—O, my back, my back! 50
Beshrew your heart for sending me about
To catch my death with jaunting up and down!
Juliet: I' faith, I am sorry that thou art not well.
Sweet, sweet, sweet nurse, tell me, what says my love?
Nurse: Your love says, like an honest gentleman, and a 55
courteous, and a kind, and a handsome, and, I warrant,
a virtuous,—Where is your mother?
Juliet: Where is my mother! why, she is within;
Where should she be? How oddly thou repliest!
"Your love says, like an honest gentleman, 60
'Where is your mother?'"
Nurse: O God's lady dear!
Are you so hot? Marry, come up, I trow;
Is this the poultice for my aching bones?
Henceforward do your messages yourself.
Juliet: Here's such a coil! Come, what says Romeo? 65
Nurse: Have you got leave to go to shrift to-day?
Juliet: I have.

70   *wanton:* uncontrolled

71   *They'll . . . scarlet:* They (your cheeks) will turn red

74   *bird's:* i.e., Juliet's

Nurse: Then hie you hence to Friar Laurence' cell;
    There stays a husband to make you a wife.
    Now comes the wanton blood up in your cheeks,   70
    They'll be in scarlet straight at any news.
    Hie you to church; I must another way,
    To fetch a ladder, by the which your love
    Must climb a bird's nest soon when it is dark.
    I am the drudge and toil in your delight,   75
    But you shall bear the burthen soon at night.
    Go; I'll to dinner; hie you to the cell.
Juliet: Hie to high fortune! Honest nurse, farewell.
                                    [*Exeunt.*]

Act 2, Scene 5: Activities

1. What creates the tremendous tension in this scene?

2. Examine Juliet's opening soliloquy (lines 1-17). First, paraphrase each line of the speech into modern *standard* English. Convert this version into modern English *slang*. Next, select appropriate background music and read both pieces to the class. Analyse what you have learned about the English language from this activity.

3. What do you learn about Juliet from the conversation between her and the Nurse? Predict how these characteristics might affect a lasting relationship between Juliet and Romeo.

4. Is the Nurse enjoying the adventure of the young people's plan to elope, or do you believe that she really wants them to be happy? What do you think Juliet believes?

5. At this point in the relationship between Romeo and Juliet, which of the two do you believe is really in control of the wedding plans? What dimension does this add to the characters of both Romeo and Juliet? If you could speak to Juliet, what would you say to her? Record your response as a speech that you could fit into the scene or as a piece of advice that you could send her in a letter.

6. How is this scene like one in a television soap opera? Write a modern exchange that would work in a television soap opera sequence.

For the next scene . . .

What does the expression, "love is blind," mean to you? What is your reaction to teenagers getting married?

Act 2, Scene 6

In this scene . . .

In this scene, Romeo, ecstatic in his love, is cautioned by Friar Laurence to show moderation. Juliet enters, and the two lovers confess their love for each other. The Friar prepares to perform the wedding ceremony.

1   *So smile the heavens:* may the heavens so smile upon and bless (this marriage)

2   *after hours:* the future

4   *countervail:* counterbalance; *exchange of joy:* that is, for the grief the future may bring

6   *close:* join

10   *powder:* gunpowder

11   *kiss:* come together. The figure is of an early cannon being fired by touching a flame from match to powder.

11-12   *The sweetest . . . deliciousness:* Too much sweetness can sicken a person.

13   *confounds:* destroys

15   *too swift . . . slow:* he who goes too quickly arrives no faster than he who goes too slowly – like the hare and the tortoise in the fable.

18   *gossamer:* filmy spider's web

19   *idles:* moves gently; *wanton:* playful

20   *vanity:* vain delight, the trivial pursuit of love

21   *ghostly:* spiritual

23   *As much . . . much:* Let me also greet him so that his thanks will not be more than I deserve.

26   *blazon:* describe it colourfully. To blazon is to describe a coat-of-arms.

26-27   *sweeten . . . air:* Let your joy be expressed in sweet words on the surrounding air. *music's tongue:* the music of your voice

29   *encounter:* meeting

Scene 6

Friar Laurence's cell.

Enter Friar Laurence and Romeo.

Friar Laurence: So smile the heavens upon this holy act,
   That after hours with sorrow chide us not!
Romeo: Amen, amen! but come what sorrow can,
   It cannot countervail the exchange of joy
   That one short minute gives me in her sight.   5
   Do thou but close our hands with holy words,
   Then love-devouring Death do what he dare;
   It is enough I may but call her mine.
Friar Laurence: These violent delights have violent ends,
   And in their triumph die, like fire and powder,   10
   Which as they kiss consume. The sweetest honey
   Is loathsome in his own deliciousness,
   And in the taste confounds the appetite;
   Therefore, love moderately; long love doth so;
   Too swift arrives as tardy as too slow.   15
   [*Enter Juliet.*]
   Here comes the lady. O, so light a foot
   Will ne'er wear out the everlasting flint.
   A lover may bestride the gossamer
   That idles in the wanton summer air,
   And yet not fall; so light is vanity.   20
Juliet: Good even to my ghostly confessor.
Friar Laurence: Romeo shall thank thee, daughter, for us
      both.
Juliet: As much to him, else is his thanks too much.
Romeo: Ah, Juliet, if the measure of thy joy
   Be heap'd like mine and that thy skill be more   25
   To blazon it, then sweeten with thy breath
   This neighbour air, and let rich music's tongue
   Unfold the imagined happiness that both
   Receive in either by this dear encounter.

30-31   *Conceit . . . ornament:* Imagination, when it is concerned with thoughts of love too deep to express in words, knows that it is the substance of love, rather than fine words about it, that matters.

32   *worth:* wealth

Juliet: Conceit, more rich in matter than in words,   30
    Brags of his substance, not of ornament.
    They are but beggars that can count their worth;
    But my true love is grown to such excess
    I cannot sum up sum of half my wealth.
Friar Laurence: Come, come with me, and we will make
      short work;   35
    For, by your leaves, you shall not stay alone
    Till Holy Church incorporate two in one.

                                          [Exeunt.]

Act 2, Scene 6: Activities

1. Do you consider Friar Laurence's caution to Romeo and his observations on lovers in general to be valid under the circumstances?

2. The actual marriage ceremony is not shown in the play. What do you imagine occurred at the ceremony? Insert a description of the ceremony and some lines of dialogue at the end of this scene. How would you costume this wedding scene?

3. Marriage is a symbolic ceremony. What is the symbolism associated with weddings? Why is this wedding surrounded by a sense of foreboding? How is this sense of foreboding conveyed to the audience?

4. If you were staging a production of *Romeo and Juliet*, would you consider the end of this scene to be a logical place to have an intermission? Why or why not?

Act 2: Consider the Whole Act

1. At what point in this act were you convinced that Romeo and Juliet were *really* in love with each other? What convinced you?

2. Imagine yourself as a practising diagnostic physician. Romeo and/or Juliet's love, or infatuation, is, in your opinion, a disease. What would you describe as the symptoms of this disease? What drug could you prescribe that might cure it or at least lessen its symptoms? How does this drug work? In what ways does the cured person differ from the sick one? If you were describing this disease in a medical journal, what name would you assign to it? As a follow-up to your article, what preven-

tative measures would you advise others to use so that they could avoid contracting the disease?

In your journal write your answer to the following questions:
- Do you suffer from any of the symptoms you have described? If so, which ones?
- Would you take your own prescribed cure? Why or why not?

Prepare a script for a segment of a newscast called "The Doctor Says" in which you have one minute to present this subject to your viewers. Present your script to the class.

3. Create a personalized horoscope for both Romeo and Juliet based on information you obtained from this act. There are many examples of horoscopes in newspapers and magazines that you can use as models. If Romeo and Juliet had read the horoscopes, would they have done anything differently? In your journal, tell whether or not you believe in horoscope predictions. Has any prediction ever come true for you? If so, write about it.

4. By now you will have begun to develop some strong reactions to the characters you have met in the play so far. Write a paper in which you respond to one or more of the following statements:
- The character I would most like to meet is . . . because . . .
- What puzzles me most about Romeo and Juliet's love scenes is . . .
- My initial impression of Friar Laurence is . . .
- What I enjoyed/disliked about Scene . . . was . . .
- My impression of . . . has changed the most because of . . .

5. Each actor must feel a sense of role when presenting a character to an audience. Choose one character and select a speech of at least ten lines from this act that you think reveals his or her personality. Rehearse

the speech and deliver it to the other members of your group. Your objective is to present a thoroughly developed character. The following checklist may help you:

- What kind of person am I?
- How do I want the audience to respond to me?
- What makes me different from the other characters in the scene?
- How do I feel when I am delivering this speech?

The checklist can be used by other members of your group to determine how well you conveyed your role. Discuss with the members of your group the differences between your role portrayal and their interpretation of it.

6. *Make a video*
   Choose a short speech, perhaps one of Romeo or Juliet's speeches in Scene 2 or a conversation between them. Working in pairs or small groups, use the camera to create a mood. Remember to rehearse the speech or speeches several times to be sure that you are clear about the meaning of the lines and the words, the movement, if any, of the characters, and the interactions that are occurring. Remember that different camera angles will create different moods. Similarly, light and colour can also alter moods and convey particular feelings.

   Prepare a shooting script or storyboard in which you do the following:
   - Consider the distance between the camera and the subject that would be appropriate for each shot. Changing the distance will change the size of the subject and the balance of what is in the shot, thereby altering the mood.
   - Determine the kind of lighting you think will best convey the mood you are seeking to create.
   - Use sound effects (musical or otherwise) to support your visual images.
   - Decide on the angles you think will be most effective in carrying the mood you want to sustain.

- Provide one visual shot per complete thought. This format will help provide clarity.
- Use pauses. Silence can be very important in conveying emotion in audio-visual presentations. Gestures are also important.
- Design an audio lead-in of appropriate music to set the scene before the visual portion actually begins. The scene could be ended in the same manner.

Now you are ready to shoot. Let the rest of the class judge how successful you have been in conveying mood through your audio-visual presentation of a scene segment.

For the next scene . . .

In your journal, record your group's responses to the following:
- What are some things that could cause a fight between two people your age?
- Describe a person you know who is always looking for a fight. What are his/her characteristics?
- Describe a person you know who never wants to fight under any circumstances. What are his/her characteristics?
- What conversation might occur between a person seeking a fight and a person wishing to avoid a fight? What argument finally decides whether they do or do not fight?
- How do you feel about fighting as a way of settling differences?

Act 3, Scene 1

In this scene . . .

Mercutio accuses Benvolio of being hot-tempered and spoiling for a fight. Tybalt enters looking for Romeo, but is ready to fight anyone. Mercutio confronts Tybalt. Romeo enters and, since it is just after his marriage, is filled with love even for his "enemy" Tybalt. Tybalt challenges Romeo, and Mercutio intervenes on Romeo's behalf. Mercutio is killed when Romeo attempts to come between the two combatants and avert the fight. Shortly afterwards, Romeo draws on Tybalt and kills him. Romeo flees to the cries of the angry citizens who are outraged at yet another outbreak of the Montague-Capulet feud. At this moment, the Prince arrives and, in anger, decrees Romeo banished. He further declares that Romeo will be killed on sight if he is found within the walls of Verona.

2   *The day is hot:* It was believed that hot weather aggravated emotions.

6   *me:* used here for emphasis

8   *by the . . . cup:* by the time the second drink begins to work on him

9   *drawer:* tapster, the person who pours liquor in a tavern

11   *Jack:* general term for a man (usually said with contempt); *in thy mood:* when you are angry

12   *soon moved to be moody:* easily provoked to anger

13   *moody to be moved:* ill-humoured enough to be provoked

14   *And what to?:* And moved to what action?

23   *as addle:* until it has become rotten (also, empty, muddled, or scrambled)

27   *fall out:* quarrel

28   *before Easter:* Easter was the time for wearing new fashions

29   *tutor me for:* instruct me in

Act 3, Scene 1

A public place.

Enter Mercutio, Benvolio, Page,
and Servants.

Benvolio: I pray thee, good Mercutio, let's retire.
The day is hot, the Capulets abroad,
And, if we meet, we shall not 'scape a brawl,
For now these hot days is the mad blood stirring.
Mercutio: Thou art like one of those fellows that when he   5
enters the confines of a tavern claps me his sword upon
the table and says, "God send me no need of thee!"
and by the operation of the second cup draws him on
the drawer, when indeed there is no need.
Benvolio: Am I like such a fellow?   10
Mercutio: Come, come, thou art as hot a Jack in thy mood
as any in Italy, and as soon moved to be moody, and
as soon moody to be moved.
Benvolio: And what to?
Mercutio: Nay, an there were two such, we should have none   15
shortly, for one would kill the other. Thou! why,
thou wilt quarrel with a man that hath a hair more, or
a hair less, in his beard, than thou hast. Thou wilt
quarrel with a man for cracking nuts, having no other
reason but because thou hast hazel eyes. What eye   20
but such an eye would spy out such a quarrel? Thy
head is as full of quarrels as an egg is full of meat,
and yet thy head hath been beaten as addle as an egg
for quarrelling. Thou hast quarrelled with a man
for coughing in the street, because he hath wakened   25
thy dog that hath lain asleep in the sun. Didst thou not
fall out with a tailor for wearing his new doublet
before Easter? with another, for tying his new shoes
with old riband? And yet thou wilt tutor me for
quarrelling!   30

32   *fee-simple:* To hold property in fee-simple was to have outright possession of it.

32-33   *should buy . . . quarter:* might have complete ownership of my life for promising that I might live an hour and a quarter. That is, so quarrelsome a person could not expect to live long.

34   *O simple!:* What a feeble joke!

36   *By my heel:* "heel" is a reference to fleeing from, "to take heel," i.e., to run away (Mercutio will stand his ground.)

44   *thou consort'st:* you keep company with

46   *Consort!:* a company of musicians who must play in musical harmony. Mercutio, trying to anger Tybalt, purposely misunderstands him. He takes "consort" in its other meaning – combine in musical harmony – and pretends that Tybalt has insulted him by calling him a hired musician (minstrel).

51   *reason coldly:* argue calmly

55   *my man:* the man I am looking for

56   *wears your livery:* Mercutio again deliberately misunderstands, taking "man" for "servant."

57   *to field:* to the duelling field

59   *can afford:* will allow me to use

62-63   *appertaining rage . . . greeting:* the anger that would be the appropriate response to such a greeting as "villain"

64   *thou know'st me not:* You do not know that by my marriage to Juliet I am related to you.

65   *Boy:* a term used with great contempt; *injuries:* insults

68   *devise:* imagine

Benvolio: An I were so apt to quarrel as thou art, any man
    should buy the fee-simple of my life for an hour and
    a quarter.
Mercutio: The fee-simple! O simple!
Benvolio: By my head, here come the Capulets.   35
Mercutio: By my heel, I care not.
    [*Enter Tybalt and others.*]
Tybalt: Follow me close, for I will speak to them.
    Gentlemen, good den; a word with one of you.
Mercutio: And but one word with one of us? Couple it with
    something; make it a word and a blow.   40
Tybalt: You shall find me apt enough to that, sir, an you
    will give occasion.
Mercutio: Could you not take some occasion without giving?
Tybalt: Mercutio, thou consort'st with Romeo,—
Mercutio: Consort! what, dost thou make us minstrels?   45
    An thou make minstrels of us, look to hear nothing
    but discords. Here's my fiddle-stick; here's that shall
    make you dance. 'Zounds, consort!
Benvolio: We talk here in the public haunt of men.
    Either withdraw unto some private place,   50
    Or reason coldly of your grievances,
    Or else depart; here all eyes gaze on us.
Mercutio: Men's eyes were made to look, and let them gaze;
    I will not budge for no man's pleasure, I.
    [*Enter Romeo.*]
Tybalt: Well, peace be with you, sir; here comes my man.   55
Mercutio: But I'll be hang'd, sir, if he wear your livery.
    Marry, go before to field, he'll be your follower;
    Your worship in that sense may call him "man."
Tybalt: Romeo, the love I bear thee can afford
    No better term than this: thou art a villain.   60
Romeo: Tybalt, the reason that I have to love thee
    Doth much excuse the appertaining rage
    To such a greeting. Villain am I none;
    Therefore farewell; I see thou know'st me not.
Tybalt: Boy, this shall not excuse the injuries   65
    That thou hast done me; therefore turn and draw.
Romeo: I do protest, I never injured thee,
    But love thee better than thou canst devise

70   *tender:* regard tenderly, value, hold dearly

73   *alla stoccata:* an Italian fencing term meaning a rapier thrust. Roughly, Mercutio, in his disgust, means that Tybalt's quarrelsome nature and known skill in fencing have made Romeo cowardly.

74   *rat-catcher:* cat, a reference to the name "Tybalt" (cat); *will you walk?:* that is, to the duelling field, will you fight a duel?

76-77   *nine lives:* a reference to the common saying that a cat has nine lives

77-78   *as you . . . hereafter:* according to how well you fight

78   *dry-beat:* beat you until there is no blood left in the other lives

79   *pilcher:* scabbard

80   *ears:* hilt (The sides of the hilt stick out like ears.)

84   *passado:* fencing thrust

86   *forbear:* stop

88   *bandying:* exchanging of blows, fighting

90   *A plague o' . . . houses:* Mercutio curses both the Capulets and the Montagues. He is related to neither family, so his death involves no matter of family honour. He is a victim of the feud. *sped:* done for, finished

91   *nothing:* no wound

92   *scratch:* as from a cat (to which Tybalt has been compared consistently)

93   *villain:* humble person, a servant (probably spoken kindly here)

97   *grave man:* dead man. Even when dying, Mercutio puns.

98   *peppered:* finished

101   *by the . . . arithmetic:* according to the exact rules as to time, distance, etc.

Till thou shalt know the reason of my love;
And so, good Capulet,—which name I tender   70
As dearly as mine own,—be satisfied.
Mercutio: O calm, dishonourable, vile submission!
Alla stoccata carries it away.   [*Draws.*]
Tybalt, you rat-catcher, will you walk?
Tybalt: What wouldst thou have with me?   75
Mercutio: Good king of cats, nothing but one of your nine
lives, that I mean to make bold withal, and, as you
shall use me hereafter, dry-beat the rest of the eight.
Will you pluck your sword out of his pilcher by the
ears? Make haste, lest mine be about your ears ere it be   80
out.
Tybalt: I am for you.   [*Drawing.*]
Romeo: Gentle Mercutio, put thy rapier up.
Mercutio: Come, sir, your *passado*.   [*They fight.*]
Romeo: Draw, Benvolio; beat down their weapons.   85
Gentlemen, for shame, forbear this outrage!
Tybalt, Mercutio, the Prince expressly hath
Forbid this bandying in Verona streets.
Hold, Tybalt! Good Mercutio!
                    [*Tybalt under Romeo's arm stabs Mercutio,
                                then flies with his followers.*]
Mercutio: I am hurt.
A plague o' both your houses! I am sped.   90
Is he gone, and hath nothing?
Benvolio: What, art thou hurt?
Mercutio: Ay, ay, a scratch, a scratch; marry, 'tis enough.
Where is my page? Go, villain, fetch a surgeon.
                                            [*Exit Page.*]
Romeo: Courage, man; the hurt cannot be much.
Mercutio: No, 'tis not so deep as a well, nor so wide as a   95
church-door; but 'tis enough, 'twill serve. Ask for me
to-morrow, and you shall find me a grave man. I am
peppered, I warrant, for this world. A plague o' both
your houses! 'Zounds, a dog, a rat, a mouse, a cat, to
scratch a man to death! a braggart, a rogue, a villain,   100
that fights by the book of arithmetic! Why the devil
came you between us? I was hurt under your arm.

106   *I have it:* I have received my deathblow.

107   *your houses:* In his last dying utterance, Mercutio repeats his curse, "A plague o' both your houses."

111   *slander:* This all began with Tybalt saying, "Thou art a villain" (line 60).

114   *in my temper . . . steel!:* roughly, "You have melted (dissolved) my courage."

116   *aspired:* striven towards or soared to

118   *This day's . . . depend:* an ominous prediction that this is but the first of more evil days to come

122   *respective lenity:* gentleness resulting from his knowledge that he is Tybalt's relative now, through marriage to Juliet

123   *conduct:* guide

130   *This:* my sword

132   *are up:* are aroused

133   *amazed:* dumbfounded, stupefied; *doom thee:* condemn you

135   *fortune's fool:* made a fool of by fortune, tricked by fortune

Romeo: I thought all for the best.
Mercutio: Help me into some house, Benvolio,
  Or I shall faint. A plague o' both your houses!   105
  They have made worms' meat of me. I have it,
  And soundly too—your houses!
                    [*Exeunt Mercutio and Benvolio.*]
Romeo: This gentleman, the Prince's near ally,
  My very friend, hath got his mortal hurt
  In my behalf; my reputation stain'd   110
  With Tybalt's slander,—Tybalt, that an hour
  Hath been my kinsman! O sweet Juliet,
  Thy beauty hath made me effeminate
  And in my temper soften'd valour's steel!
  [*Re-enter Benvolio.*]
Benvolio: O Romeo, Romeo, brave Mercutio's dead!   115
  That gallant spirit hath aspired the clouds,
  Which too untimely here did scorn the earth.
Romeo: This day's black fate on more days doth depend;
  This but begins the woe others must end.
  [*Re-enter Tybalt.*]
Benvolio: Here comes the furious Tybalt back again.   120
Romeo: Alive, in triumph! and Mercutio slain!
  Away to heaven, respective lenity,
  And fire-eyed fury be my conduct now!
  Now, Tybalt, take the villain back again
  That late thou gavest me; for Mercutio's soul   125
  Is but a little way above our heads,
  Staying for thine to keep him company.
  Either thou, or I, or both, must go with him.
Tybalt: Thou, wretched boy, that didst consort him here,
  Shalt with him hence.
Romeo: This shall determine that.   130
                    [*They fight; Tybalt falls.*]
Benvolio: Romeo, away, be gone!
  The citizens are up, and Tybalt slain.
  Stand not amazed; the Prince will doom thee death
  If thou art taken. Hence, be gone, away!
Romeo: O, I am fortune's fool!   135
Benvolio: Why dost thou stay?
                    [*Exit Romeo.*]

141   *discover:* reveal

142   *manage:* course

153   *nice:* trivial

156   *take truce:* make peace; *unruly spleen:* uncontrolled temper

157   *tilts:* thrusts or jabs

159   *all as hot:* equally as angry

160-163 *with one hand . . . Retorts it:* The two combatants fought with a rapier in one hand and a dagger in the other. Each one turns aside the first thrust of the other. *Retorts it:* hurls it back.

167   *an envious:* a malicious

169   *by and by:* very quickly

170   *entertain'd:* considered

[*Enter Citizens.*]
First Citizen: Which way ran he that kill'd Mercutio?
Tybalt, that murderer, which way ran he?
Benvolio: There lies that Tybalt.
First Citizen: Up, sir, go with me;
I charge thee in the Prince's name, obey.
[*Enter Prince, attended by Montague, Capulet, their Wives,
and others.*]
Prince: Where are the vile beginners of this fray?   140
Benvolio: O noble Prince, I can discover all
The unlucky manage of this fatal brawl.
There lies the man, slain by young Romeo,
That slew thy kinsman, brave Mercutio.
Lady Capulet: Tybalt, my cousin! O my brother's child!   145
O Prince! O cousin! husband! O, the blood is spilt
Of my dear kinsman! Prince, as thou art true,
For blood of ours, shed blood of Montague.
O cousin, cousin!
Prince: Benvolio, who began this bloody fray?   150
Benvolio: Tybalt, here slain, whom Romeo's hand did slay!
Romeo that spoke him fair, bid him bethink
How nice the quarrel was, and urged withal
You high displeasure; all this uttered
With gentle breath, calm look, knees humbly bow'd,   155
Could not take truce with the unruly spleen
Of Tybalt deaf to peace, but that he tilts
With piercing steel at bold Mercutio's breast,
Who, all as hot, turns deadly point to point,
And, with a martial scorn, with one hand beats   160
Cold death aside, and with the other sends
It back to Tybalt, whose dexterity
Retorts it. Romeo he cries aloud,
"Hold, friends! friends, part!" and, swifter than his
tongue,
His agile arm beats down their fatal points,   165
And 'twixt them rushes; underneath whose arm
An envious thrust from Tybalt hit the life
Of stout Mercutio, and then Tybalt fled;
But by and by comes back to Romeo,
Who had but newly entertain'd revenge,   170

176   *Affection . . . false:* He lies out of friendship for Romeo.

184   *should end:* should otherwise have ended

188   *My blood:* the blood of Mercutio, who was the Prince's relative

189   *amerce:* punish

192   *purchase out abuses:* pay for crimes

196   *Mercy . . . kill:* Murderers who are pardoned are then free to murder others and, consequently, pardon of one murder can lead to other murders.

And to 't they go like lightning, for, ere I
Could draw to part them, was stout Tybalt slain;
And, as he fell, did Romeo turn and fly.
This is the truth, or let Benvolio die.
Lady Capulet: He is a kinsman to the Montague,   175
Affection makes him false, he speaks not true.
Some twenty of them fought in this black strife,
And all those twenty could but kill one life.
I beg for justice, which thou, Prince, must give;
Romeo slew Tybalt, Romeo must not live.   180
Prince: Romeo slew him, he slew Mercutio;
Who now the price of his dear blood doth owe?
Montague: Not Romeo, Prince, he was Mercutio's friend;
His fault concludes but what the law should end,
The life of Tybalt.
Prince: And for that offence   185
Immediately we do exile him hence.
I have an interest in your hate's proceeding,
My blood for your rude brawls doth lie a-bleeding;
But I'll amerce you with so strong a fine
That you shall all repent the loss of mine.   190
I will be deaf to pleading and excuses;
Nor tears nor prayers shall purchase out abuses;
Therefore use none. Let Romeo hence in haste,
Else, when he's found, that hour is his last.
Bear hence this body and attend our will.   195
Mercy but murders, pardoning those that kill.
                                         [*Exeunt.*]

Act 3, Scene 1: Activities

1. How do you feel when Tybalt and his companions meet Benvolio and Mercutio? Does the meeting suggest what might follow? You have probably seen this same sort of situation on a current television show. How long would the scene actually be on television? Would it take longer on stage? Why or why not?

2. Tybalt always insults Mercutio. What is the nature of these insults? Would these things insult you today? Write about an incident in which you were insulted. How did you react? What did you think of the person who insulted you?

3. When Mercutio says "a plague o' both your houses," he is really voicing one of the central themes of the play. Summarize the events that make this pronouncement prophetic, and state why it is "death" to be loyal to either a Montague or a Capulet.

4. Write a newspaper feature on the Montague-Capulet fight. A feature story in a newspaper emphasizes special human interest, something that appeals to some feeling we share. In your account you should include the following:
   • how and why Tybalt provokes Mercutio
   • how Mercutio could have avoided the confrontation
   • why Romeo tried to avoid a fight
   • how Mercutio's death is really Romeo's fault
   • how Romeo takes the law into his own hands and avenges the death of his friend.

   In your feature story, include your opinion about the Prince's actions following the slaying. Comment, too, on whether the Prince could have prevented the deaths of Mercutio and Tybalt, and whether Romeo deserved what happened to him.

5. Exchange your newspaper feature with a classmate. Imagine that you are a television anchor and have just been given "copy" on the Montague-Capulet fight. You

have only one minute of airtime to fill. Which facts from the story will you include, and which facts will you eliminate? Prepare your condensed script, and deliver your story aloud to a group that includes the person whose story you began with. Discuss the way each story puts a different slant on the events.

6. Select a brief comic incident between two characters in this scene. Working with a partner, convey the main *feeling* expressed in the incident by combining a facial expression and a body action as you deliver the lines. It is helpful to recall a personal incident in which you experienced a similar feeling. Remember to discuss your presentation carefully with your partner.

7. What do you think are the qualities of true friendship? Do you think that Romeo and Mercutio share any of these qualities? Would you say that, in general, friendship is more emotional than rational? In your journal, describe your best friend and state what attracted you to him or her.

For the next scene . . .

When someone is talking to you about a subject that is very important to you and he or she suddenly begins discussing something that is seemingly unrelated, how do you react? How do you react to bad news?

Act 3, Scene 2

In this scene . . .

In a soliloquy, Juliet expresses her desire to be with Romeo. The Nurse enters and tells Juliet of the death of Tybalt and of Romeo's banishment. The scene ends with the Nurse's promise to find Romeo so that the two lovers can have a final meeting before Romeo goes into exile.

1   *steeds:* the horses that pulled the chariot of the sun god, Phoebus

2   *Phoebus' lodging:* the west, where the sun sets

3   *Phaethon:* Phoebus's son who, when allowed to drive his father's chariot for one day, could not control the horses. Because Phaeton's uncontrolled ride threatened the earth with destruction, Zeus killed him with a bolt of lightning.

6   *runaways' eyes may wink:* The sense is that Juliet wishes the day to quickly give way to night, with which she associates love and all that love implies.

10   *civil:* serious, grave

12   *learn:* teach

14   *Hood . . . cheeks:* In falconry, the hawk had a hood over its eyes until it was let fly at the game. It was "unmann'd" when it was untamed, and it "bated," or flapped its wings, when it was unhooded and was about to fly off into the air.

15–16 *till strange . . . modesty:* Until true love (love in its sexual sense) thinks courtly love (love acted) is a silly false appearance

17-19 *come, thou day . . . back:* Juliet's imaginative way of saying that the beauty of Romeo will shine out in the night

25   *garish:* glaring, gaudy

26   *I have . . . love:* I have bought Romeo's love with my love.

Scene 2

Capulet's orchard.

Enter Juliet.

Juliet: Gallop apace, you fiery-footed steeds,
Towards Phœbus' lodging; such a waggoner
As Phaethon would whip you to the west,
And bring in cloudy night immediately.
Spread thy close curtain, love-performing night,   5
That runaways' eyes may wink: and, Romeo,
Leap to these arms, untalk'd of and unseen.
Lovers can see to do their amorous rites,
By their own beauties; or, if love be blind,
It best agrees with night. Come, civil night,   10
Thou sober-suited matron, all in black,
And learn me how to lose a winning match,
Play'd for a pair of stainless maidenhoods:
Hood my unmann'd blood, bating in my cheeks,
With thy black mantle; till strange love grown bold,   15
Think true love acted simple modesty.
Come, night; come, Romeo; come, thou day in night;
For thou wilt lie upon the wings of night,
Whiter than new snow on a raven's back.
Come, gentle night, come, loving, black-brow'd night,   20
Give me my Romeo; and, when he shall die,
Take him and cut him out in little stars,
And he will make the face of heaven so fine
That all the world will be in love with night,
And pay no worship to the garish sun.   25
O, I have bought the mansion of a love,
But not possess'd it, and, though I am sold,
Not yet enjoy'd. So tedious is this day
As is the night before some festival
To an impatient child that hath new robes   30
And may not wear them. O, here comes my nurse,

34   *cords:* rope ladder: a ladder much like a conventional one except that it is made entirely of rope

40   *envious:* cruel, malicious; *Romeo can:* that is, be cruel to Tybalt

47   *cockatrice:* a fabulous creature with a rooster's head on a serpent's body. It was believed to have the power to kill by a glance.

51   *determine of my weal or woe:* will decide my joy or grief

53   *God save the mark!:* In this context the expression, the origin of which is uncertain, means, "God have mercy."

54   *corse:* corpse

56   *in gore-blood:* blood clotted; *swounded:* fainted

57   *poor bankrupt:* Having lost Romeo, Juliet is bankrupt of his love and, therefore, of all her wealth.

59   *Vile earth:* her body; *to earth resign:* be buried

60   *press . . . bier:* weigh down the one coffin, be buried together

64   *What storm . . . contrary?:* What kind of storm is this with winds from opposite directions? Up to this point, Juliet thought it was Romeo who was dead.

67   *dreadful trumpet:* the trumpet which will blow when the world ends and the Last Judgment occurs (1 Corinthians 15:52); *general doom:* Day of Judgment

And she brings news; and every tongue that speaks
But Romeo's name speaks heavenly eloquence.
[Enter Nurse, with cords.]
Now, nurse, what news? What hast thou there? the cords
That Romeo bid thee fetch?
Nurse: Ay, ay, the cords.   35
                              [Throws them down.]
Juliet: Ay me! what news? Why dost thou wring thy hands?
Nurse: Ah, well-a-day! he's dead, he's dead, he's dead!
    We are undone, lady, we are undone!
    Alack the day! he's gone, he's kill'd, he's dead!
Juliet: Can Heaven be so envious?   40
Nurse: Romeo can,
    Though Heaven cannot, O Romeo, Romeo!
    Who ever would have thought it? Romeo!
Juliet: What devil art thou, that dost torment me thus?
    This torture should be roar'd in dismal hell.
    Hath Romeo slain himself? Say thou but "I",   45
    And that bare vowel "I" shall poison more
    Than the death-darting eye of cockatrice.
    I am not I, if there be such an I;
    Or those eyes shut, that make thee answer "I."
    If he be slain, say "I"; or if not, "No".   50
    Brief sounds determine of my weal or woe.
Nurse: I saw the wound, I saw it with mine eyes,—
    God save the mark!—here on his manly breast.
    A piteous corse, a bloody piteous corse!
    Pale, pale as ashes, all bedaub'd in blood,   55
    All in gore-blood; I swounded at the sight.
Juliet: O, break, my heart! poor bankrupt, break at once!
    To prison, eyes, ne'er look on liberty!
    Vile earth, to earth resign; end motion here;
    And thou and Romeo press one heavy bier!   60
Nurse: O Tybalt, Tybalt, the best friend I had!
    O courteous Tybalt! honest gentleman!
    That ever I should live to see thee dead!
Juliet: What storm is this that blows so contrary?
    Is Romeo slaughter'd, and is Tybalt dead?   65
    My dear-loved cousin, and my dearer lord?
    Then, dreadful trumpet, sound the general doom!

77   *Despised . . . show!:* ugly material concealed in beauty

80   *what hadst . . . hell:* What business had you in hell?

81   *bower:* enclose

87   *naught:* nothing, worthless; *dissemblers:* deceivers

88   *man:* servant; *aqua vitae:* strong spirits (alcoholic beverage), such as brandy

98   *smooth thy name:* reclaim (buy back) your good name

103   *Your tributary . . . woe:* Your tears are really the property of sorrow.

For who is living, if those two are gone?
Nurse: Tybalt is gone, and Romeo banished;
   Romeo that kill'd him, he is banished.   70
Juliet: O God! did Romeo's hand shed Tybalt's blood?
Nurse: It did, it did; alas the day, it did!
Juliet: O serpent heart, hid with a flowering face!
   Did ever dragon keep so fair a cave?
   Beautiful tyrant! fiend angelical!   75
   Dove-feather'd raven! wolvish-ravening lamb!
   Despised substance of divinest show!
   Just opposite to what thou justly seem'st,
   A damned saint, an honourable villain!
   O nature, what hadst thou to do in hell,   80
   When thou didst bower the spirit of a fiend
   In mortal paradise of such sweet flesh?
   Was ever book containing such vile matter
   So fairly bound? O, that deceit should dwell
   In such a gorgeous palace!
Nurse: There's no trust,   85
   No faith, no honesty in men; all perjured,
   All forsworn, all naught, all dissemblers.
   Ah, where's my man? Give me some *aqua vitæ*;
   These griefs, these woes, these sorrows make me old.
   Shame come to Romeo!
Juliet: Blister'd be thy tongue   90
   For such a wish! he was not born to shame.
   Upon his brow shame is ashamed to sit;
   For 'tis a throne where honour may be crown'd
   Sole monarch of the universal earth.
   O, what a beast was I to chide at him!   95
Nurse: Will you speak well of him that kill'd your cousin?
Juliet: Shall I speak ill of him that is my husband?
   Ah, poor my lord, what tongue shall smooth thy name,
   When I, thy three-hours wife, have mangled it?
   But, wherefore, villain, didst thou kill my cousin?   100
   That villain cousin would have kill'd my husband.
   Back, foolish tears, back to your native spring;
   Your tributary drops belong to woe,
   Which you, mistaking, offer up to joy.
   My husband lives, that Tybalt would have slain;   105

110   *presses to:* forces itself into

114   *Hath slain . . . Tybalts:* is more difficult to bear than the death
        of ten thousand Tybalts

116   *if sour woe . . . fellowship:* if one sorrow must have another sorrow
        to keep it company

117   *needly will:* must

120   *Which . . . moved?:* news of the deaths of her parents, which
        might have aroused ordinary grief, might have been expected,
        but not the banishment of Romeo.

121   *with a rearward:* a battle image – like a rear-guard of an army
        adding its attack; that is, to follow up with

126   *In that word's death:* in the death summed up in that word
        (banishment); *sound:* express

132   *beguiled:* cheated

135   *maiden-widowed:* to die a widow without ever having really been
        a wife

139   *wot:* know

And Tybalt's dead, that would have slain my husband.
All this is comfort; wherefore weep I then?
Some word there was, worser than Tybalt's death,
That murder'd me; I would forget it fain;
But, O, it presses to my memory   110
Like damned guilty deeds to sinners' minds:
"Tybalt is dead, and Romeo—banished."
That "banished," that one word "banished,"
Hath slain ten thousand Tybalts. Tybalt's death
Was woe enough, if it had ended there;   115
Or, if sour woe delights in fellowship
And needly will be rank'd with other griefs,
Why follow'd not, when she said, "Tybalt's dead,"
Thy father, or thy mother, nay, or both,
Which modern lamentation might have moved?   120
But with a rearward following Tybalt's death,
"Romeo is banished," to speak that word,
Is father, mother, Tybalt, Romeo, Juliet,
All slain, all dead. "Romeo is banished!"
There is no end, no limit, measure, bound,   125
In that word's death; no words can that woe sound.
Where is my father and my mother, nurse?
Nurse: Weeping and wailing over Tybalt's corse.
    Will you go to them? I will bring you thither.
Juliet: Wash they his wounds with tears; mine shall be spent, 130
    When theirs are dry, for Romeo's banishment.
    Take up those cords. Poor ropes, you are beguiled,
    Both you and I, for Romeo is exiled.
    He made you for a highway to my bed,
    But I, a maid, die maiden-widowed.   135
    Come cords; come, nurse; I'll to my wedding-bed;
    And death, not Romeo, take my maidenhead!
Nurse: Hie to your chamber. I'll find Romeo
    To comfort you; I wot well where he is.
    Hark ye, your Romeo will be here at night.   140
    I'll to him; he is hid at Laurence' cell.
Juliet: O, find him! Give this ring to my true knight,
    And bid him come to take his last farewell.
                                        [Exeunt.]

Act 3, Scene 2: Activities

1. Reread Juliet's first speech at the beginning of this scene. On one side of a page, list all the references she makes to day, and on the other side of the page, list all the references she makes to night. Include in your lists the qualities that Juliet associates with each. Decide what the purpose of this contrast is. Then rehearse a reading of the speech. Try to give proper emphasis to Juliet's language so that your reading conveys a clear impression to your audience. Be prepared to read your rehearsed speech to the class. Remember to use body movement and voice modulation during your reading.

2. In your journal, write about an incident in which you didn't do something because you had a "bad feeling" about it. Juliet has a premonition (a feeling or warning that something is going to happen) in this scene, just as Romeo did before he attended the Capulet party. Decide what Romeo and Juliet fear about these warnings. Why do they both choose to ignore the warnings? Share your findings with your group.

3. Look up the word "banished" in a dictionary and list as many meanings as you can. In groups, decide why Juliet keeps repeating the word. How many of your listed definitions might apply to Juliet's situation? Write a note in which you explain to a friend the significance of being banished in Romeo and Juliet's time.

4. Extreme emotional stress is very difficult to handle. In groups, decide what stresses Juliet experiences. How does she deal with them? Write a paper describing how you might have reacted in similar circumstances.

5. In groups, improvise a reading of the dialogue between the Nurse and Juliet. Interpret the lines and determine how they might be spoken to reveal clearly the characters and theme. Present your readings to the class. Decide

what makes each presentation different and which reading you found most effective. Make a detailed note of your findings in your journal.

6. Divide a page in half vertically. Make a list of your impressions of Tybalt. Beside the list, record Juliet's impression of him. Are there similarities and/or differences? Explain to a partner how this comparison either does or does not change your opinion of Tybalt. What agreements have you reached?

7. In your journal, make a list of any words or phrases that you particularly like from Juliet's speeches in this scene and explain why you chose them. How could you incorporate them in your everyday vocabulary? Keep a record of how you do this.

For the next scene . . .

In your opinion, how much of what you learn in school really prepares you for situations that you encounter in real life? How helpful have people been who have given you advice about the way you should handle a difficult problem? Relate an incident to prove your point.

Act 3, Scene 3

In this scene . . .

This scene between the Friar and Romeo shows Romeo's grief at the sudden turn of events in his life. The Friar expresses the hope that Romeo's banishment will not be permanent and that the two lovers will be reunited in happiness. The Nurse enters and conveys the news of Juliet's grief and turmoil to Romeo, who threatens to kill himself. The Friar proposes a plan whereby Romeo can argue that he killed Tybalt out of self-defence. The Friar then devises a way for Romeo to escape to Mantua, where he will be safe until all the difficulties can be resolved.

1   *fearful:* literally, full of fear; horrible, dreadful

2   *Affliction . . . parts:* Sorrow has fallen in love with your qualities.

4   *doom:* sentence

5   *craves . . . hand:* wishes to know me

9   *dooms-day:* death (the Day of Judgment)

10   *vanish'd:* issued, came from

17   *without:* outside

21   *mis-term'd:* misnamed

24   *deadly sin:* ingratitude

25   *calls death:* looks on as punishable by death

26   *rush'd:* brushed

Scene 3

Friar Laurence's cell.

Enter Friar Laurence.

Friar Laurence: Romeo, come forth; come forth, thou fearful
    man:
    Affliction is enamour'd of thy parts,
    And thou art wedded to calamity.
    [Enter Romeo.]
Romeo: Father, what news? What is the Prince's doom?
    What sorrow craves acquaintance at my hand,   5
    That I yet know not?
Friar Laurence: Too familiar
    Is my dear son with such sour company.
    I bring thee tidings of the Prince's doom.
Romeo: What less than dooms-day is the Prince's doom?
Friar Laurence: A gentler judgment vanish'd from his lips,   10
    Not body's death, but body's banishment.
Romeo: Ha, banishment! Be merciful, say "death";
    For exile hath more terror in his look,
    Much more than death. Do not say "banishment!"
Friar Laurence: Here from Verona art thou banished.   15
    Be patient, for the world is broad and wide.
Romeo: There is no world without Verona walls,
    But purgatory, torture, hell itself.
    Hence banished is banish'd from the world,
    And world's exile is death; then "banished"   20
    Is death mis-term'd. Calling death "banished,"
    Thou cut'st my head off with a golden axe,
    And smilest upon the stroke that murders me.
Friar Laurence: O deadly sin! O rude unthankfulness!
    Thy fault our law calls death; but the kind prince,   25
    Taking thy part, hath rush'd aside the law,

28   *dear:* true

33   *validity:* value

34   *More honourable state:* a condition leading to greater honour; *more courtship:* nearer to court life or better chances for romantic pursuits (affairs)

35   *carrion-flies:* flies that live on dead flesh

38   *Who:* which; *vestal:* virginal

48   *Howlings attend it:* It is accompanied by howls of anguish and despair.

49   *ghostly confessor:* an unseen hearer of confessions

51   *mangle:* wound

52   *fond:* foolish

55   *Adversity's . . . philosophy:* Philosophy makes misfortune bearable.

59   *Displant:* remove from one location to another; in this context, move Verona from where it is to where I am going

63   *dispute:* discuss; *estate:* condition

And turn'd that black word death to banishment.
This is dear mercy, and thou seest it not.
Romeo: 'Tis torture, and not mercy. Heaven is here,
Where Juliet lives; and every cat and dog   30
And little mouse, every unworthy thing,
Live here in heaven and may look on her;
But Romeo may not. More validity,
More honourable state, more courtship lives
In carrion-flies than Romeo; they may seize   35
On the white wonder of dear Juliet's hand
And steal immortal blessings from her lips,
Who, even in pure and vestal modesty,
Still blush, as thinking their own kisses sin;
But Romeo may not; he is banished.   40
This may flies do, when I from this must fly;
They are free men, but I am banished:
And say'st thou yet that exile is not death?
Hadst thou no poison mix'd, no sharp-ground knife,
No sudden mean of death, though ne'er so mean,   45
But "banished" to kill me?—"Banished"?
O friar, the damned use that word in hell;
Howlings attend it. How hast thou the heart,
Being a divine, a ghostly confessor,
A sin-absolver, and my friend profess'd,   50
To mangle me with that word "banished"?
Friar Laurence: Thou fond mad man, hear me but speak
    a word.
Romeo: O, thou wilt speak again of banishment.
Friar Laurence: I'll give thee armour to keep off that word;
Adversity's sweet milk, philosophy,   55
To comfort thee, though thou art banished.
Romeo: Yet "banished"? Hang up philosophy!
Unless philosophy can make a Juliet,
Displant a town, reverse a prince's doom,
It helps not, it prevails not. Talk no more.   60
Friar Laurence: O, then I see that madmen have no ears.
Romeo: How should they, when that wise men have no eyes?
Friar Laurence: Let me dispute with thee of thy estate.
Romeo: Thou canst not speak of that thou dost not feel.

70   *Taking . . . grave:* stretched out as I shall soon be in my grave

75   *taken:* captured

77   *simpleness:* foolishness, stupidity

85   *woeful sympathy:* shared misery

90   *so deep an O:* such deep grief (as in the feeling of emptiness or nothingness); "O" is a symbol for nothing.

Wert thou as young as I, Juliet thy love,   65
An hour but married, Tybalt murdered,
Doting like me and like me banished,
Then mightst thou speak, then mightst thou tear thy hair,
And fall upon the ground, as I do now,
Taking the measure of an unmade grave.   70
                                        [Knocking within.]
Friar Laurence: Arise; one knocks. Good Romeo, hide
    thyself.
Romeo: Not I; unless the breath of heart-sick groans,
    Mist-like, infold me from the search of eyes.
                                              [Knocking.]
Friar Laurence: Hark, how they knock! Who's there? Romeo,
    arise;
    Thou wilt be taken.—Stay a while!—Stand up;   75
                                              [Knocking.]
    Run to my study.—By and by!—God's will,
    What simpleness is this!—I come, I come!
                                              [Knocking.]
    Who knocks so hard? Whence come you? What's your
        will?
Nurse [Within.] Let me come in, and you shall know my
    errand.
    I come from Lady Juliet.
    [Enter Nurse.]
Friar Laurence: Welcome, then.   80
Nurse: O holy friar, O, tell me, holy friar,
    Where is my lady's lord, where's Romeo?
Friar Laurence: There on the ground, with his own tears
    made drunk.
Nurse: O, he is even in my mistress' case,
    Just in her case!
Friar Laurence: O woeful sympathy!   85
    Piteous predicament!
Nurse: Even so lies she,
    Blubbering and weeping, weeping and blubbering.
    Stand up, stand up; stand, an you be a man.
    For Juliet's sake, for her sake, rise and stand.
    Why should you fall into so deep an O?   90

94   *old:* toughened or hardened

98   *My conceal'd lady:* my secret wife (their marriage is secret);
        cancell'd: crossed out, eliminated, erased, obliterated

103   *level:* aim

106   *anatomy:* body

107   *sack:* destroy, leave in total ruin

108   *mansion:* body

109   *cries out:* proclaims

112   *Unseemly . . . man:* In form you are a man, but your conduct is
        totally unbecoming of a man. A woman wouldn't act this way.
        (In Elizabethan times, women were not considered equal to men.)

113   *Or . . . both!:* or a hideous creature with the form of a man and
        the nature of a woman

115   *temper'd:* mixed

118   *damned hate:* an act of hate, suicide, that will damn your soul
        for eternity

119   *Why rail'st . . . earth?:* Why do you curse your birth, the heaven
        and the earth?

120   *do meet:* have a part, come together

122   *wit:* good sense

123   *Which . . . in all:* You put all your good qualities to shame by
        misusing them in the same way a miser does his wealth. *usurer:*
        a person who lends money at exhorbitant interest

126   *form of wax:* a figure made of wax, i.e., human only in form but
        without feeling

127   *digressing:* differing, straying, departing

Romeo: Nurse!
Nurse: Ah, sir! ah, sir! Death's the end of all.
Romeo: Spakest thou of Juliet? How is it with her?
    Doth she not think me an old murderer,
    Now I have stain'd the childhood of our joy   95
    With blood removed but little from her own?
    Where is she? and how doth she? and what says
    My conceal'd lady to our cancell'd love?
Nurse: O, she says nothing, sir, but weeps and weeps;
    And now falls on her bed; and then starts up,   100
    And Tybalt calls; and then on Romeo cries,
    And then down falls again.
Romeo: As if that name,
    Shot from the deadly level of a gun,
    Did murder her, as that name's cursed hand
    Murder'd her kinsman. O, tell me, friar, tell me,   105
    In what vile part of this anatomy
    Doth my name lodge? Tell me, that I may sack
    The hateful mansion.   *[Drawing his sword.]*
Friar Laurence: Hold thy desperate hand!
    Art thou a man? Thy form cries out thou art:
    Thy tears are womanish; thy wild acts denote   110
    The unreasonable fury of a beast.
    Unseemly woman in a seeming man,
    Or ill-beseeming beast in seeming both!
    Thou hast amazed me. By my holy order,
    I thought thy disposition better temper'd.   115
    Hast thou slain Tybalt? Wilt thou slay thyself,
    And slay thy lady that in thy life lives,
    By doing damned hate upon thyself?
    Why rail'st thou on thy birth, the heaven, and earth?
    Since birth, and heaven, and earth, all three do meet   120
    In thee at once, which thou at once wouldst lose.
    Fie, fie, thou shamest thy shape, thy love, thy wit;
    Which, like a usurer, abound'st in all,
    And usest none in that true use indeed
    Which should bedeck thy shape, thy love, thy wit.   125
    Thy noble shape is but a form of wax,
    Digressing from the valour of a man;

128   *hollow perjury:* a false and empty lie

129   *Killing:* should you kill; *that love:* the love for Juliet

130   *Thy wit . . . love:* your good sense which should make your good looks and your love much better

131   *Mis-shapen . . . both:* distorted in its lack of consideration for your looks and your feelings of love

134   *dismember'd:* blown to pieces, totally destroyed; *with thine own defence:* by the intelligence that should have protected you

130–34   *Thy wit . . . defence:* The sense of these lines is that Romeo's intelligence, which should enhance his body and his love, has failed to guide either, and like the powder in an unskilled or untrained soldier's powder-flask, is set on fire through his own ignorance and blows him up instead of protecting him.

137   *happy:* fortunate

144   *pout'st upon:* look upon with displeasure

147   *Ascend:* climb up, by the ladder given to Juliet

148   *till the watch be set:* till the watchmen go on duty at the city gates

149   *pass:* leave Verona

151   *blaze:* make public

157   *apt unto:* ready for, prepared to do

160   *what learning is!:* How wonderful learning is. (The Nurse is astonished at the Friar's wisdom because she hasn't had the privilege of formal education.

166   *state:* fortune

Thy dear love sworn but hollow perjury,
Killing that love which thou hast vow'd to cherish;
Thy wit, that ornament to shape and love,   130
Mis-shapen in the conduct of them both,
Like powder in a skilless soldier's flask,
Is set a-fire by thine own ignorance,
And thou dismember'd with thine own defence.
What, rouse thee, man! thy Juliet is alive,   135
For whose dear sake thou wast but lately dead:
There art thou happy. Tybalt would kill thee,
But thou slew'st Tybalt: there art thou happy too.
The law that threaten'd death becomes thy friend
And turns it to exile: there art thou happy.   140
A pack of blessings light upon thy back;
Happiness courts thee in his best array;
But, like a misbehaved and sullen wench,
Thou pout'st upon thy fortune and thy love.
Take heed, take heed, for such die miserable.   145
Go, get thee to thy love, as was decreed;
Ascend her chamber; hence and comfort her.
But look thou stay not till the watch be set,
For then thou canst not pass to Mantua,
Where thou shalt live till we can find a time   150
To blaze your marriage, reconcile your friends,
Beg pardon of the Prince, and call thee back
With twenty hundred thousand times more joy
Than thou went'st forth in lamentation.
Go before, nurse; commend me to thy lady,   155
And bid her hasten all the house to bed,
Which heavy sorrow makes them apt unto.
Romeo is coming.
Nurse: O Lord, I could have stay'd here all the night
To hear good counsel. O, what learning is!   160
My lord, I'll tell my lady you will come.
Romeo: Do so, and bid my sweet prepare to chide.
Nurse: Here, sir, a ring she bid me give you, sir.
Hie you, make haste, for it grows very late.   *[Exit.]*
Romeo: How well my comfort is revived by this!   165
Friar Laurence: Go hence; good-night; and here stands all
    your state:

171   *hap:* happening, event

173   *But:* were it not that; *joy past joy:* the joy of seeing Juliet

174   *so brief:* so hastily, so abruptly

Either be gone before the watch be set,
Or by the break of day disguised from hence.
Sojourn in Mantua; I'll find out your man,
And he shall signify from time to time   170
Every good hap to you that chances here.
Give me thy hand; 'tis late. Farewell; good-night.
Romeo: But that a joy past joy calls out on me,
It were a grief, so brief to part with thee.
Farewell.   *[Exeunt.]* 175

Act 3, Scene 3: Activities

1. Is Juliet's state of mind in Scene 2 the same as Romeo's in this scene? Decide what that state of mind is and what has caused it. In your journal, make a note explaining how you would feel in similar circumstances.

2. Friar Laurence doesn't seem to be getting the response he wants from Romeo in this scene. Decide what is wrong with the Friar's approach and alter it so that it's more effective. In pairs, read your speech to the person role-playing Romeo. What is Romeo's response?

3. What do you think is the purpose of bringing the Nurse and Friar Laurence together in this scene? Could it have been done differently? If so, how would you have done it?

4. How accurate is the Nurse's account of Juliet's mental state (lines 99–102)?

5. In groups, discuss the reason why Romeo contemplates suicide. What advice would you give him at this point? As a friend, how would you present the advice to him?

6. Some people have suggested that Friar Laurence is a "benign conspirator." Determine what you think this term means. What is the real motivation behind the Friar's decision to help the lovers? Does the Friar hope to gain something by intervening in the Montague–Capulet problems?

7. Why do you think the Nurse wants to assist Romeo and Juliet? Should she be doing this? If you had any advice to offer the Nurse, what would it be?

8. In groups, brainstorm and make a list of Romeo's mood swings so far in the play, and label them positive or negative. Are these mood swings typical of a teenager?

You may wish to write your reaction as a private journal entry. Write a note outlining how you might help Romeo to "smooth out" his emotional responses to situations.

For the next scene . . .

Who do you think should make decisions about *your* future? Do you think that women and men have the same opportunities to determine their own futures?

Act 3, Scene 4

In this scene . . .

In this scene, Capulet declares that Paris will marry Juliet on Thursday. He assumes that Juliet will obey his wishes; he doesn't know that she is already married.

1   *fall'n out:* happened, occurred

2   *move:* persuade, urge

6   *promise:* assure; *but for:* had it not been for

11   *mew'd up . . . heaviness:* shut up with her grief

12   *make . . . tender:* be so forward as to make an offer

16   *son:* son-in-law. Capulet is so certain of Juliet's acceptance that he already calls Paris "son."

18   *soft!:* Wait a moment.

20   *O':* on

23   *keep no great ado:* not go to much trouble

25   *held him carelessly:* did not hold him in very high regard, hadn't much respect for him

Scene 4

A room in Capulet's house.

*Enter Capulet, Lady Capulet, and
Paris.*

Capulet: Things have fall'n out, sir, so unluckily
  That we have had no time to move our daughter.
  Look you, she loved her kinsman Tybalt dearly,
  And so did I. Well, we were born to die.
  'Tis very late, she'll not come down to-night;   5
  I promise you, but for your company,
  I would have been a-bed an hour ago.
Paris: These times of woe afford no time to woo.
  Madam, good-night; commend me to your daughter.
Lady Capulet: I will, and know her mind early to-morrow;   10
  To-night she's mew'd up to her heaviness.
Capulet: Sir Paris, I will make a desperate tender
  Of my child's love. I think she will be ruled
  In all respects by me; nay, more, I doubt it not.
  Wife, go you to her ere you go to bed;   15
  Acquaint her here of my son Paris' love;
  And bid her, mark you me, on Wednesday next—
  But, soft! what day is this?
Paris: Monday, my lord.
Capulet: Monday! ha, ha! Well, Wednesday is too soon,
  O' Thursday let it be,—o' Thursday, tell her,   20
  She shall be married to this noble earl.
  Will you be ready? Do you like this haste?
  We'll keep no great ado—a friend or two;
  For, hark you, Tybalt being slain so late,
  It may be thought we held him carelessly,   25
  Being our kinsman, if we revel much;
  Therefore we'll have some half a dozen friends,
  And there an end. But what say you to Thursday?

32   *against:* in readiness for, in time for

35   *by and by:* very soon now

Paris: My lord, I would that Thursday were to-morrow.
Capulet: Well, get you gone; o' Thursday be it, then.   30
    Go you to Juliet, ere you go to bed;
    Prepare her, wife, against this wedding-day.
    Farewell, my lord. Light to my chamber, ho!
    Afore me! it is so very very late
    That we may call it early by and by.   35
    Good-night.   *[Exeunt.]*

Act 3, Scene 4: Activities

1. What is revealed about Paris when he says, "These times of woe afford no time to woo?" Why would Paris say this? If you could speak to Paris at this point, what would you say to him? In pairs, role-play the situation you have devised.

2. Tybalt's death has greatly affected Capulet's wedding plans. Decide whether you believe Capulet's actions concerning the wedding are appropriate under the circumstances. Write him a letter expressing these views.

3. Discuss what the Capulet wedding festivities might look like. Consider the following:
   • How might Juliet dress?
   • How might Paris dress?
   • Where would the wedding be held?
   • How would the wedding customs differ from our own?
   • What might the wedding reception be like?
   • How would you stage the wedding scene?

4. In groups, decide whether or not you think Paris is the right choice of husband for Juliet. Write a letter to him offering advice or guidance.

5. Create a character profile of Capulet and one of Lady Capulet by writing your impressions of them in this scene and in Act 1, Scene 1. What is your assessment of the relationship that exists between the two of them? Do they act like a typical married couple?

6. Do you think the Capulets needed help understanding their daughter? Write to them as a friend giving your opinion,

7. In groups, determine whether or not Juliet should have told her parents the truth about what she had done, instead of deceiving them. If she had told the truth, what do you think would have been the outcome?

For the next scene . . .

All of us have had arguments with our parents that we couldn't win. How have you reacted when this happened to you? Occasionally, parents become upset and annoyed when they feel they are not communicating with a teenager. What kinds of things do parents say under these circumstances?

Act 3, Scene 5

In this scene . . .

Romeo and Juliet part after spending one night together. Lady Capulet recounts her version of Tybalt's slaying, declaring that the Capulets will have vengeance for the death of one of their kin. She says that Romeo is in Mantua and that she will have him killed. She then announces that Juliet is to marry Paris on Thursday. Juliet rejects the marriage, and her father threatens her with banishment from the family. The Nurse advises Juliet to go along with the wishes of her family. Juliet refuses and decides to go to Friar Laurence for help.

3   *fearful:* apprehensive, full of fear

7   *envious streaks:* spiteful, harmful "streaks" of daylight

8   *severing:* the clouds break away before the light

9   *Night's candles:* the stars

13   *exhales:* draws out. The Elizabethans believed that the sun draws up (exhales) gases from the earth and sets fire to them, producing shooting stars (meteors).

19   *morning's eye:* the sun

20   *reflex:* reflection; *Cynthia:* the moon

23   *care:* wish

28   *Straining . . . sharps:* straining her voice for the notes and thus producing "sharps" (shrill notes)

29   *division:* melody

Scene 5

Capulet's orchard.

Enter Romeo and Juliet, above,
at the window.

Juliet: Wilt thou be gone? it is not yet near day.
  It was the nightingale, and not the lark,
  That pierced the fearful hollow of thine ear;
  Nightly she sings on yond pomegranate-tree.
  Believe me, love, it was the nightingale.   5
Romeo: It was the lark, the herald of the morn,
  No nightingale. Look, love, what envious streaks
  Do lace the severing clouds in yonder east.
  Night's candles are burnt out, and jocund day
  Stands tiptoe on the misty mountain tops.   10
  I must be gone and live, or stay and die.
Juliet: Yond light is not day-light, I know it, I;
  It is some meteor that the sun exhales,
  To be to thee this night a torch-bearer,
  And light thee on thy way to Mantua;   15
  Therefore stay yet; thou need'st not to be gone.
Romeo: Let me be ta'en, let me be put to death;
  I am content, so thou wilt have it so.
  I'll say yon grey is not the morning's eye,
  'Tis but the pale reflex of Cynthia's brow;   20
  Nor that is not the lark, whose notes do beat
  The vaulty heaven so high above our heads.
  I have more care to stay than will to go.
  Come, death, and welcome! Juliet wills it so.
  How is 't, my soul? Let's talk; it is not day.   25
Juliet: It is, it is! Hie hence, be gone, away!
  It is the lark that sings so out of tune,
  Straining harsh discords and unpleasing sharps.
  Some say the lark makes sweet division;
  This doth not so, for she divideth us.   30

31 *Some . . . eyes:* It was a popular belief that, since the toad's eyes are more beautiful than those of the lark, the two had exchanged eyes.

33 *Since arm . . . affray:* since that voice frightens us from each other's arms

34 *hunt's-up:* an early morning song to arouse the hunters

46 *much in years:* far along in life

54 *ill-divining:* foreboding evil, ill, or malice

59 *Dry . . . blood:* It was an old belief that sighing drained the blood from the heart and that, as a result, the person appeared pale, as in death.

61-62 *what dost . . . faith?:* Why have you anything to do with Romeo, who is totally different from you?

68 *procures her hither:* causes her to come here

Some say the lark and loathed toad change eyes;
O, now I would they had changed voices too!
Since arm from arm that voice doth us affray,
Hunting thee hence with hunt's-up to the day.
O, now be gone; more light and light it grows.   35
Romeo: More light and light; more dark and dark our woes!
[Enter Nurse.]
Nurse: Madam!
Juliet: Nurse?
Nurse: Your lady mother is coming to your chamber.
    The day is broke; be wary, look about.   *[Exit.]*   40
Juliet: Then, window, let day in, and let life out.
Romeo: Farewell, farewell! One kiss, and I'll descend.
                                    [Romeo descends.]
Juliet: Art thou gone so! Love, lord, ay, husband, friend!
    I must hear from thee every day in the hour,
    For in a minute there are many days.   45
    O, by this count I shall be much in years
    Ere I again behold my Romeo!
Romeo: Farewell!
    I will omit no opportunity
    That may convey my greetings, love, to thee.   50
Juliet: O, think'st thou we shall ever meet again?
Romeo: I doubt it not; and all these woes shall serve
    For sweet discourses in our time to come.
Juliet: O God, I have an ill-divining soul!
    Methinks I see thee, now thou art below,   55
    As one dead in the bottom of a tomb.
    Either my eyesight fails, or thou look'st pale.
Romeo: And trust me, love, in my eye so do you;
    Dry sorrow drinks our blood. Adieu, adieu!   *[Exit.]*
Juliet: O Fortune, Fortune! all men call thee fickle;   60
    If thou art fickle, what dost thou with him
    That is renown'd for faith? Be fickle, Fortune;
    For then, I hope, thou wilt not keep him long,
    But send him back.
Lady Capulet: [Within.] Ho, daughter! are you up?   65
Juliet: Who is 't that calls? Is it my lady mother?
    Is she not down so late, or up so early?
    What unaccustom'd cause procures her hither?

69   *how now:* What is wrong?

74   *wit:* good sense. Thus, the meaning is that too much sorrow always indicates lack of good sense.

75   *feeling:* heartfelt

90   *runagate:* law-breaker

91   *unaccustom'd dram:* a drink (that is, poison) different from what he is accustomed to

98   *temper:* mix

102   *wreak:* revenge

[Enter Lady Capulet.]
Lady Capulet: Why, how now, Juliet?
Juliet: Madam, I am not well.
Lady Capulet: Evermore weeping for your cousin's death?   70
What, wilt thou wash him from his grave with tears?
An if thou couldst, thou couldst not make him live;
Therefore, have done. Some grief shows much of love,
But much of grief shows still some want of wit.
Juliet: Yet let me weep for such a feeling loss.   75
Lady Capulet: So shall you feel the loss, but not the friend
Which you weep for.
Juliet: Feeling so the loss,
I cannot choose but ever weep the friend.
Lady Capulet: Well, girl, thou weep'st not so much for his
death,
As that the villain lives which slaughter'd him.   80
Juliet: What villain, Madam?
Lady Capulet: That same villain, Romeo.
Juliet: [Aside.] Villain and he be many miles asunder.—
God pardon him! I do, with all my heart;
And yet no man like he doth grieve my heart.
Lady Capulet: That is, because the traitor murderer lives.   85
Juliet: Ay, madam, from the reach of these my hands.
Would none but I might venge my cousin's death!
Lady Capulet: We will have vengeance for it, fear thou not;
Then weep no more. I'll send to one in Mantua,
Where that same banish'd runagate doth live,   90
Shall give him such an unaccustom'd dram,
That he shall soon keep Tybalt company;
And then, I hope, thou wilt be satisfied.
Juliet: Indeed, I never shall be satisfied
With Romeo, till I behold him—dead—   95
Is my poor heart, so for a kinsman vex'd.
Madam, if you could find out but a man
To bear a poison, I would temper it
That Romeo should, upon receipt thereof,
Soon sleep in quiet. O, how my heart abhors   100
To hear him named, and cannot come to him,
To wreak the love I bore my cousin
Upon his body that hath slaughter'd him!

106   *needy time:* time that needs happiness

110   *sorted out:* chosen

130   *a conduit:* a fountain

132   *Thou counterfeits:* You imitate; *bark:* a boat

133   *still:* always

135   *flood:* sea

137   *Without:* unless there is; *overset:* capsize

Lady Capulet: Find thou the means, and I'll find such
    a man.
  But now I'll tell thee joyful tidings, girl.   105
Juliet: And joy comes well in such a needy time.
  What are they, I beseech your ladyship?
Lady Capulet: Well, well, thou hast a careful father, child;
  One who, to put thee from thy heaviness,
  Hath sorted out a sudden day of joy,   110
  That thou expect'st not nor I look'd not for.
Juliet: Madam, in happy time, what day is that?
Lady Capulet: Marry, my child, early next Thursday morn,
  The gallant, young, and noble gentleman,
  The County Paris, at Saint Peter's Church,   115
  Shall happily make thee there a joyful bride.
Juliet: Now, by Saint Peter's Church and Peter too,
  He shall not make me there a joyful bride.
  I wonder at this haste; that I must wed
  Ere he that should be husband comes to woo.   120
  I pray you, tell my lord and father, madam,
  I will not marry yet; and, when I do, I swear,
  It shall be Romeo, whom you know I hate,
  Rather than Paris. These are news indeed!
Lady Capulet: Here comes your father; tell him so yourself, 125
  And see how he will take it at your hands.
  [Enter Capulet and Nurse.]
Capulet: When the sun sets, the air doth drizzle dew;
  But for the sunset of my brother's son
  It rains downright.
  How now! a conduit, girl? What, still in tears?   130
  Evermore showering? In one little body
  Thou counterfeits a bark, a sea, a wind:
  For still thy eyes, which I may call the sea,
  Do ebb and flow with tears; the bark thy body is,
  Sailing in this salt flood; the winds, thy sighs: 135
  Who, raging with thy tears, and they with them,
  Without a sudden calm, will overset
  Thy tempest-tossed body. How now, wife!
  Have you deliver'd to her our decree?
Lady Capulet: Ay, sir; but she will none, she gives you
    thanks.   140

142   *take me with you:* Let me understand you.

145   *wrought:* brought about

147   *Not proud . . . have:* I am not pleased that you have done this, but I can show gratitude for your reasons for doing it.

149   *meant:* intended for

150   *chop-logic!:* a person who argues over fine points

152   *Mistress minion:* a bold or outspoken woman

154   *fettle:* prepare; *'gainst:* in readiness for

156   *hurdle:* a cart equipped with runners used for drawing condemned people to the gallows where they were hanged

158   *tallow-face:* pale or waxen faced, therefore, cowardly or afraid

165   *itch:* itch to hit you

169   *hilding:* good for nothing, useless person

170   *rate:* to berate, to scold, to bring out the bad points of

172   *smatter:* chatter, that is, your bits (smatterings) of wisdom

175   *gravity:* wise advice; *o'er . . . bowl:* among your friends as you drink together

I would the fool were married to her grave!
Capulet: Soft! take me with you, take me with you, wife.
How! will she none? Doth she not give us thanks?
Is she not proud? Doth she not count her blest,
Unworthy as she is, that we have wrought   145
So worthy a gentleman to be her bridegroom?
Juliet: Not proud, you have; but thankful that you have.
Proud can I never be of what I hate;
But thankful even for hate, that is meant love.
Capulet: How now! how now! chop-logic! What is this?   150
"Proud," and "I thank you," and "I thank you not;"
And yet "not proud." Mistress minion, you
Thank me no thankings, nor proud me no prouds;
But fettle your fine joints 'gainst Thursday next,
To go with Paris to Saint Peter's Church,   155
Or I will drag thee on a hurdle thither.
Out, you green-sickness carrion! Out, you baggage!
You tallow-face!
Lady Capulet: Fie, fie, what, are you mad?
Juliet: Good father, I beseech you on my knees,
Hear me with patience but to speak a word.   160
Capulet: Hang thee, young baggage! disobedient wretch!
I tell thee what: get thee to church o'Thursday,
Or never after look me in the face.
Speak not, reply not, do not answer me!
My fingers itch. Wife, we scarce thought us blest   165
That God had lent us but this only child;
But now I see this one is one too much,
And that we have a curse in having her.
Out on her, hilding!
Nurse: God in heaven bless her!
You are to blame, my lord, to rate her so.   170
Capulet: And why, my lady wisdom? Hold your tongue,
Good prudence; smatter with your gossips, go.
Nurse: I speak no treason.
Capulet: O, God ye god-den.
Nurse: May not one speak?
Capulet: Peace, you mumbling fool!
Utter your gravity o'er a gossip's bowl;   175
For here we need it not.

177   *God's bread!:* by the bread of the holy sacrament

182   *demesnes:* domains or properties

183   *Stuff'd:* full of; *parts:* qualities

184   *Proportion'd . . . man:* every part in harmony with all other parts, as in the ideal man

185   *puling:* whining, snivelling, or sickly

186   *mammet:* doll; *in her fortune's tender:* when such good fortune is offered to her

191   *do not use:* am not used (accustomed)

192   *advise:* be advised, or, think about this carefully

197   *be forsworn:* break my oath; go back on what I have said now and on my promise to Paris

211   *stratagems:* plans or schemes for playing cruel tricks

Lady Capulet: You are too hot.

Capulet: God's bread! it makes me mad.

    Day, night, hour, tide, time, work, play,
    Alone, in company, still my care hath been
    To have her match'd; and having now provided   180
    A gentleman of noble parentage,
    Of fair demesnes, youthful and nobly train'd,
    Stuff'd, as they say, with honourable parts,
    Proportion'd as one's thought would wish a man;
    And then to have a wretched puling fool,   185
    A whining mammet, in her fortune's tender,
    To answer, "I'll not wed; I cannot love,
    I am too young; I pray you, pardon me."
    But, an you will not wed, I'll pardon you.
    Graze where you will, you shall not house with me.   190
    Look to 't, think on 't, I do not use to jest.
    Thursday is near; lay hand on heart, advise.
    An you be mine, I'll give you to my friend;
    An you be not, hang, beg, starve, die in the streets,
    For, by my soul, I'll ne'er acknowledge thee,   195
    Nor what is mine shall never do thee good.
    Trust to 't, bethink you; I'll not be forsworn.   *[Exit.]*

Juliet: Is there no pity sitting in the clouds,
    That sees into the bottom of my grief?
    O, sweet my mother, cast me not away!   200
    Delay this marriage for a month, a week;
    Or, if you do not, make the bridal bed
    In that dim monument where Tybalt lies.

Lady Capulet: Talk not to me, for I'll not speak a word.
    Do as thou wilt, for I have done with thee.   *[Exit.]* 205

Juliet: O God!—O nurse, how shall this be prevented?
    My husband is on earth, my faith in heaven;
    How shall that faith return again to earth,
    Unless that husband send it me from heaven
    By leaving earth? Comfort me, counsel me!   210
    Alack, alack, that heaven should practise stratagems
    Upon so soft a subject as myself!
    What say'st thou? Hast thou not a word of joy?
    Some comfort, nurse.

Nurse: Faith, here it is.

215   *all the world to nothing:* I'll bet anything

216   *challenge you:* claim you (as his wife)

221   *dishclout:* dishcloth, usually dirty in those days

222   *green:* green eyes were considered desirable; *quick:* alive or lively

223   *Beshrew my very heart:* Curse my heart indeed.

229   *Amen!:* So be what you say (to the Nurse's curse).

235   *Ancient damnation!:* Devilish old creature!

236   *to wish me:* for her to wish me

239   *counsellor:* that is, the Nurse, who had so often advised her

241   *remedy:* solution for this problem

Romeo is banish'd; and all the world to nothing,   215
That he dares ne'er come back to challenge you;
Or, if he do, it needs must be by stealth.
Then, since the case so stands as now it doth,
I think it best you married with the County.
O, he's a lovely gentleman!   220
Romeo's a dishclout to him. An eagle, madam,
Hath not so green, so quick, so fair an eye
As Paris hath. Beshrew my very heart,
I think you are happy in this second match,
For it excels your first; or if it did not,   225
Your first is dead; or 'twere as good he were,
As living here and you no use of him.
Juliet: Speakest thou from thy heart?
Nurse: And from my soul too;
Or else beshrew them both.
Juliet: Amen!
Nurse: What?
Juliet: Well, thou hast comforted me marvellous much.   230
Go in; and tell my lady I am gone,
Having displeased my father, to Laurence' cell,
To make confession and to be absolved.
Nurse: Marry, I will; and this is wisely done   *[Exit.]*
Juliet: Ancient damnation! O most wicked fiend!   235
Is it more sin to wish me thus forsworn,
Or to dispraise my lord with that same tongue
Which she hath praised him with above compare
So many thousand times? Go, counsellor;
Thou and my bosom henceforth shall be twain.   240
I'll to the friar, to know his remedy;
If all else fail, myself have power to die.   *[Exit.]*

Act 3, Scene 5: Activities

1. Romeo and Juliet talk about their relationship and again use night and day images. Why do they seem to prefer darkness over light?

2. Select several words and phrases that appeal to you from the speeches between Romeo and Juliet. Use them in a paragraph describing the parting of two modern-day lovers.

3. What evidence is there that Juliet believes her destiny and that of Romeo are somehow controlled by fate? What other events in the play could support this view?

4. If Romeo had approached the Capulet family and asked forgiveness for his part in Tybalt's death, would he have been forgiven? What evidence supports your view?

5. Frequently, teenagers don't want to reveal their true feelings to their parents. In your journal, relate an incident in which you hid your true feelings. In groups, discuss how and why Juliet hides her feelings from her parents. Is she lying? Explain your answer.

6. From what you know of Capulet, what kind of father do you think he is? Put yourself in the scene and write a speech telling Capulet what you think about his relationship with his daughter. Act out your speech for your group.

7. What possible reasons could Lady Capulet have for cursing her daughter as she does in line 141? Make a list of other memorable oxymorons (linking of opposites) in this scene. In groups, decide what is the value of using this device in a play.

8. In groups, brainstorm and list the characteristics of the Nurse that you have noted so far. Has your opinion of her changed in this scene? Discuss whether or not you would have acted the same way she did.

9. Is there something Juliet might have done in this scene to postpone her marriage to Paris? Was there an opportunity she missed? Write a letter to Juliet explaining what strategies she might have used to avoid the ugly confrontation with her parents.

Or

Write the letter to a friend who is having difficulties with parents, using Juliet's situation as an example of what can happen.

Act 3: Consider the Whole Act

1. Write a paper in which you respond to two or three of the following questions, situations, or statements:
   - In my opinion, the real cause of the street brawl was . . . because . . .
   - I would like to know more about what motivated . . . (a character) to . . .
   - What I really don't understand in this act is . . .
   - I have changed my mind about . . . (a character) because . . .
   - What I really enjoyed in this act was . . .
   - The character I really can't figure out is . . . .

2. Create a wanted poster listing Romeo as one of Verona's Ten Most Wanted Criminals. Explain the crime of which he is accused. Give a physical description of him, including details of clothing worn when he was last seen. Give any other information that might help in identifying the wanted man. Design a finished poster that conveys the above information clearly, effectively, and with impact. You might work with an artist in the class to help you prepare a drawing of the subject, suitably labelled to aid in identification.

3. Stage a part of the fight scene between Mercutio and Tybalt. Make sure that action and dialogue fit together. Limit the segment to about three minutes of activity time

so the desired impact is achieved and the mood is sustained. When preparing this segment, remember the following:

- The movement and grouping you plan are visually important because they can "set up" the audience for the fight before it begins.
- Remember to "get into character" well before you stage the segment.
- Plan your posture exactly, according to the character's mood, age, and attitude toward other people on the stage.
- Make sure you rehearse every move so your action looks real and believable.
- Block out your movements and rehearse several times before you make your presentation.

Remember to first discuss with your group the segment you are going to present. In particular, discuss the characters, their moods, and their expected responses to situations. Rehearse your dialogue carefully. You can judge your success by the responses of the other members of your class.

4. Write a column for a newspaper or a magazine in which you use the events of this act to illustrate that parents are often the unintentional causes of what they perceive as their children's bad behaviour. Suggest some ideas that adults could follow to make relationships between teenagers and adults more productive.

5. Working with a partner, select a major event involving two people from this act. Decide what is the main idea and the mood of the event. Then, decide how to stage this event. Plan your stage setting, entrances, exits, and the props you will need. Your object is to make the rest of the class see and feel your message. Keep the following in mind:
- Be as spontaneous as you can.
- Become your character.
- Play off your partner's acting.

- Show your character's emotions.
- Speak loudly and clearly.
- Move naturally and freely.
- Don't hurry your lines.

6. Record as many famous family feuds from history and the present as you can. Find out:
   - what caused these feuds
   - how long the feuds lasted
   - what the consequences of the feuds were on the community at large
   - how the feuds ended.

   Consider what similarities there are between the feuds you have researched and the Montague-Capulet feud. What ways can you suggest to help end a feud? Follow the independent study format suggested in the activities for Act 1, Scene 1 (page 27) when you undertake this project.

For the next scene . . .

Describe a situation in which you have taken desperate measures to avoid doing something you really didn't want to do.

Act 4, Scene 1

In this scene . . .

Paris and Juliet finally meet at the Friar's cell. Paris is
there to arrange his marriage to Juliet, and Juliet is
there seeking the Friar's aid in preventing the marriage.
Friar Laurence gives Juliet a potion to drink that will
give her the appearance of death. The Friar also has
a plan that will allow Romeo to rescue Juliet from
the tomb and take her to Mantua.

There is much dramatic irony in the exchanges
between Juliet and Paris in this scene. Dramatic irony
occurs when the words or actions of a speaker in a
play carry a meaning that is not intended by the
speaker but is understood by the audience and, often,
by another character. The irony results from the contrast
between the meaning intended by the speaker and
the added significance seen by others.

3   *And . . . haste:* And I shall not get in the way of his haste by being slow myself.

5   *Uneven is the course:* The road is winding; that is, the procedure is highly irregular.

8   *Venus smiles not:* love does not grow and prosper

10   *sway:* control

12   *inundation:* flood

13   *too much . . . alone:* receiving too much attention when she is by herself

14   *society:* association with another or others

20   *That may be must be:* It has been decreed that you shall be my wife.

21   *a certain text:* a saying to rely on

27   *of more price:* worth more

Act 4, Scene 1

Friar Laurence's cell.

Enter Friar Laurence and Paris.

Friar Laurence: On Thursday, sir? The time is very short.
Paris: My father Capulet will have it so;
   And I am nothing slow, to slack his haste.
Friar Laurence: You say you do not know the lady's mind.
   Uneven is the course, I like it not.   5
Paris: Immoderately she weeps for Tybalt's death,
   And therefore have I little talk'd of love,
   For Venus smiles not in a house of tears.
   Now, sir, her father counts it dangerous
   That she doth give her sorrow so much sway,   10
   And in his wisdom hastes our marriage
   To stop the inundation of her tears,
   Which, too much minded by herself alone,
   May be put from her by society.
   Now do you know the reason of this haste.   15
Friar Laurence: [Aside.] I would I knew not why it should
   be slow'd.
   Look, sir, here comes the lady towards my cell.
   [Enter Juliet.]
Paris: Happily met, my lady and my wife!
Juliet: That may be, sir, when I may be a wife.
Paris: That may be must be, love, on Thursday next.   20
Juliet: What must be shall be.
Friar Laurence: That's a certain text.
Paris: Come you to make confession to this father?
Juliet: To answer that, I should confess to you.
Paris: Do not deny to him that you love me.
Juliet: I will confess to you that I love him.   25
Paris: So will you, I am sure, that you love me.
Juliet: If I do so, it will be of more price,
   Being spoke behind your back, than to your face.

29   *abused:* marred, spoiled

36   *for it is not mine own:* She means it is Romeo's.

41   *God shield:* God forbid

42   *will I rouse ye:* that is, for the wedding

47   *It strains . . . wits:* To find a solution is beyond the reach of
      my wits.

48   *prorogue:* postpone

53   *resolution:* decision (to die by her own hand)

54   *help it presently:* help prevent it immediately

57   *label:* seal attached by a slip of paper to a legal deed; *to another
      deed:* the marriage to Paris

59   *This:* the dagger or knife; *both:* heart and hand

60   *long-experienced time:* many years of experience

62   *extremes:* extreme sufferings; *bloody:* capable of shedding blood

63   *play the umpire:* decide whether I shall continue to suffer or
      end my suffering by death

64   *commission:* authority

67   *If what . . . remedy:* if what you say does not offer some way
      out of my problem

Paris: Poor soul, thy face is much abused with tears.
Juliet: The tears have got small victory by that,   30
  For it was bad enough before their spite.
Paris: Thou wrong'st it, more than tears, with that report.
Juliet: That is no slander, sir, which is a truth;
  And what I spake, I spake it to my face.
Paris: Thy face is mine, and thou hast slander'd it.   35
Juliet: It may be so, for it is not mine own.
  Are you at leisure, holy father, now;
  Or shall I come to you at evening mass?
Friar Laurence: My leisure serves me, pensive daughter,
    now.
  My Lord, we must entreat the time alone.   40
Paris: God shield I should disturb devotion!
  Juliet, on Thursday early will I rouse ye;
  Till then, adieu; and keep this holy kiss.   *[Exit.]*
Juliet: O, shut the door! and when thou hast done so,
  Come weep with me, past hope, past cure, past help!   45
Friar Laurence: Ah, Juliet, I already know thy grief;
  It strains me past the compass of my wits.
  I hear thou must, and nothing may prorogue it,
  On Thursday next be married to this County.
Juliet: Tell me not, friar, that thou hear'st of this,   50
  Unless thou tell me how I may prevent it.
  If, in thy wisdom, thou canst give no help,
  Do thou but call my resolution wise,
  And with this knife I'll help it presently.
  God join'd my heart and Romeo's, thou our hands;   55
  And ere this hand, by thee to Romeo's seal'd,
  Shall be the label to another deed,
  Or my true heart with treacherous revolt
  Turn to another, this shall slay them both.
  Therefore, out of thy long-experienced time,   60
  Give me some present counsel, or, behold,
  'Twixt my extremes and me this bloody knife
  Shall play the umpire, arbitrating that
  Which the commission of thy years and art
  Could to no issue of true honour bring.   65
  Be not so long to speak; I long to die
  If what thou speak'st speak not of remedy.

69   *craves . . . execution:* demands desperate measures in the carrying out

74   *chide:* clear

75   *That copest . . . from it:* you who are ready to encounter death to avoid marrying Paris

79   *in thievish ways:* where thieves wait in hiding

81   *charnel-house:* a vault where the bones or bodies of the dead are piled

83   *reeky shanks:* rotting, foul-smelling legs; *chapless:* from which the jaws have fallen

91   *look:* make certain

96   *a cold . . . humour:* a cold fluid producing sleep

97   *his native . . . surcease:* its natural activity, but will cease to beat

100   *paly:* wan; *eyes' windows:* eyelids

102   *supple government:* the control that keeps it supple

104   *borrow'd:* counterfeit or false

105   *two and forty hours:* probably from Tuesday night to Thursday night, when she will awaken in the tomb

Friar Laurence: Hold, daughter! I do spy a kind of hope,
   Which craves as desperate an execution
   As that is desperate which we would prevent,   70
   If, rather than to marry County Paris,
   Thou hast the strength of will to slay thyself,
   Then is it likely thou wilt undertake
   A thing like death to chide away this shame,
   That copest with death himself to 'scape from it;   75
   And, if thou darest, I'll give thee remedy.
Juliet: O, bid me leap, rather than marry Paris,
   From off the battlements of yonder tower,
   Or walk in thievish ways, or bid me lurk
   Where serpents are; chain me with roaring bears,   80
   Or shut me nightly in a charnel-house,
   O'er-cover'd quite with dead men's rattling bones,
   With reeky shanks and yellow chapless skulls;
   Or bid me go into a new-made grave
   And hide me with a dead man in his shroud—   85
   Things that, to hear them told, have made me tremble;
   And I will do it without fear or doubt,
   To live an unstain'd wife to my sweet love.
Friar Laurence: Hold, then. Go home, be merry, give consent
   To marry Paris. Wednesday is to-morrow.   90
   To-morrow night look that thou lie alone;
   Let not thy nurse lie with thee in thy chamber.
   Take thou this vial, being then in bed,
   And this distilled liquor drink thou off;
   When presently through all thy veins shall run   95
   A cold and drowsy humour; for no pulse
   Shall keep his native progress, but surcease;
   No warmth, no breath, shall testify thou livest;
   The roses in thy lips and cheeks shall fade
   To paly ashes, thy eyes' windows fall,   100
   Like death, when he shuts up the day of life;
   Each part, deprived of supple government,
   Shall, stiff and stark and cold, appear like death:
   And in this borrow'd likeness of shrunk death
   Thou shalt continue two and forty hours,   105
   And then awake as from a pleasant sleep.
   Now, when the bridegroom in the morning comes

110   *uncover'd:* The custom was to leave the corpse's face uncovered.

113   *against:* in anticipation of the time when; in readiness for the
        time when

114   *drift:* purpose, plan

119   *inconstant toy:* fickle fancy; that is, some trick your mind plays
        on you

120   *Abate:* make weak, diminish; *valour:* courage (in carrying out
        the plan)

122   *prosperous:* successful

125   *afford:* make it happen

To rouse thee from thy bed, there art thou dead.
Then, as the manner of our country is,
In thy best robes uncover'd on the bier   110
Thou shalt be borne to that same ancient vault
Where all the kindred of the Capulets lie.
In the mean time, against thou shalt awake,
Shall Romeo by my letters know our drift,
And hither shall he come; and he and I   115
Will watch thy waking, and that very night
Shall Romeo bear thee hence to Mantua.
And this shall free thee from this present shame,
If no inconstant toy, nor womanish fear,
Abate thy valour in the acting it.   120
Juliet: Give me, give me! O, tell not me of fear!
Friar Laurence: Hold; get you gone, be strong and prosperous
In this resolve, I'll send a friar with speed
To Mantua, with my letters to thy lord.
Juliet: Love give me strength! and strength shall help afford.   125
Farewell, dear father!   *[Exeunt.]*

Act 4, Scene 1: Activities

1. In groups, discuss and record your response to the following question: Why has it taken such a long time for Paris and Juliet to meet?

2. Paris confesses to the Friar that he is in a great hurry to marry Juliet. In groups, decide what reasons Paris has for his haste and determine why the Friar doesn't attempt to talk him out of the marriage. If you were the Friar, what would you have done? Discuss how the Friar's actions could affect the outcome of the play. Make a journal entry of the results of your discussion. At the end of the play, reread this entry and see if you still agree with it.

3. Create a profile of Paris based on your impressions of him in this scene. If you are male, would you want Paris as a friend? If you are female, would you date him? Record your responses in your journal.

4. In groups, discuss whether or not Juliet is being fair when she talks to Paris in this scene. Discuss the way you would have handled a similar situation or encounter. Write a brief note to Juliet commenting on her behaviour.

5. This scene has many double entendres (meanings). Make double columns on a page. List Paris's statements on the right and Juliet's replies on the left. Is it possible to show that the two of them are really discussing the same problem but from different perspectives? Who do you think handles the situation better, Juliet or Paris? What is the advantage of using this technique?

6. In groups, discuss why you think Friar Laurence decides to intervene in a domestic dispute about which he really appears to know very little. Note your conclusions in your journal.

7. Some directors find the conversation between Friar Laurence and Juliet rather boring. In groups, discuss what alterations you might make to the text to make the encounter more appealing to a modern audience. Prepare an updated script and present it to another group for evaluation. Select the best script and present it in performance to the whole class.

8. When a writer uses an image, he or she tries to make the reader see, feel, or imagine a picture. Writers know that every individual will respond to an image in his or her own way. In groups, make a list of the most obvious images in this scene (ten entries should be enough). Decide what the key image is. Discuss whether it is possible to over-use an image. Could a writer deliberately over-use an image? Do you think that Shakespeare has over-used an image in this scene? (Remember that much of Shakespeare's audience was basically illiterate and there may have been an advantage in repeating an image.) In this age of television and video, can you think of any programs that make use of repeated images for effect? Share your findings with your group.

For the next scene . . .

Imagine yourself in a situation in which all of the choices you have are unpleasant. You realize that you must take charge of your life. What would you do?

Act 4, Scene 2

In this scene . . .

Capulet makes wedding preparations, and Juliet returns from her meeting with Friar Laurence. As part of the plan devised by the Friar, she pretends to agree to her father's wishes. At the end of the scene, Juliet and the Nurse retire to Juliet's room to prepare the clothing and jewelry she will wear on her wedding day. Capulet rejoices at Juliet's change in attitude.

2   *cunning:* talented or highly skilled

3   *none ill:* no bad cooks; *try:* test

4   *lick their fingers:* taste their own cooking

8   *goes not:* does not get a job

10   *unfurnish'd:* unprepared

14   *peevish:* obstinate; *harlotry:* silly wench; *it:* used in contempt, instead of "she"

15   *shrift:* confession

16   *gadding:* wandering about idly

19   *behests:* commands; *enjoin'd:* commanded or required

26   *becomed:* becoming, seemly

Scene 2

Hall in Capulet's house.

Enter Capulet, Lady Capulet,
Nurse, and two Serving-men.

Capulet: So many guests invite as here are writ.

         [Exit First Servant.]

 Sirrah, go hire me twenty cunning cooks.

Second Servant: You shall have none ill, sir; for I'll try if

 they can lick their fingers.

Capulet: How canst thou try them so?   5

Second Servant: Marry, sir, tis an ill cook that cannot lick

 his own fingers; therefore he that cannot lick his fingers

 goes not with me.

Capulet: Go, be gone.   *[Exit Second Servant.]*

 We shall be much unfurnish'd for this time.   10

 What, is my daughter gone to Friar Laurence?

Nurse: Ay, forsooth.

Capulet: Well, he may chance to do some good on her.

 A peevish self-will'd harlotry it is.

 [Enter Juliet.]

Nurse: See where she comes from shrift with merry look. 15

Capulet: How now, my headstrong! where have you been

 gadding?

Juliet: Where I have learn'd me to repent the sin

 Of disobedient opposition

 To you and your behests, and am enjoin'd

 By holy Laurence to fall prostrate here,   20

 To beg your pardon. Pardon, I beseech you!

 Henceforward I am ever ruled by you.

Capulet: Send for the County; go tell him of this:

 I'll have this knot knit up to-morrow morning.

Juliet: I met the youthful lord at Laurence' cell,   25

 And gave him what becomed love I might,

 Not stepping o'er the bounds of modesty.

32   *bound:* indebted

33   *closet:* chamber, room

34   *sort:* select

35   *to furnish me:* for me to wear

43-44 *What, ho! . . . forth:* He calls to the servants, who are not around.

47   *reclaim'd:* brought back into the fold

Capulet: Why, I am glad on 't; this is well; stand up.
 This is as 't should be. Let me see the County;
 Ay, marry, go, I say, and fetch him hither.   30
 Now, afore God! this reverend holy friar,
 All our whole city is much bound to him.
Juliet: Nurse, will you go with me into my closet,
 To help me sort such needful ornaments
 As you think fit to furnish me to-morrow?   35
Lady Capulet: No, not till Thursday; there is time enough.
Capulet: Go, nurse, go with her; we'll to church to-
  morrow.   *[Exeunt Juliet and Nurse.]*
Lady Capulet: We shall be short in our provision;
 'Tis now near night.
Capulet: Tush, I will stir about,
 And all things shall be well, I warrant thee, wife; 40
 Go thou to Juliet, help to deck up her.
 I'll not to bed to-night; let me alone;
 I'll play the housewife for this once. What, ho!
 They are all forth. Well, I will walk myself
 To County Paris, to prepare him up   45
 Against to-morrow. My heart is wondrous light,
 Since this same wayward girl is so reclaim'd.
          [Exeunt.]

Act 4, Scene 2: Activities

1. Why do you think the wedding day is pushed ahead from Thursday to Wednesday?

2. Old Capulet seems to make all the wedding preparations without consulting anyone else. In groups, decide why he is so preoccupied with this aspect of the wedding. Insert a dialogue between Capulet and his wife in which Lady Capulet attempts to include some of her own preferences. Who wins the argument? How does the loser react? In pairs, present your dialogue to your group or to the whole class.

3. In groups, discuss whether or not you think Capulet really believes Juliet's sudden change of heart to be "ever ruled" by him. Consider whether or not the exchange between father and daughter adds anything to your knowledge of either of the two characters. In your opinion, is it really necessary for Juliet to lie to her father?

4. If you could speak to Capulet at this point about his treatment of his daughter, what would you say to him? Write an article, using this scene as a basis for outlining the way fathers should treat their daughters. Address your article to present-day parents.

5. In your journal, recount an incident in which you or someone you know lied. What were the consequences of the lie? Write a short letter to Juliet advising her of the consequences of telling a lie.

For the next scene . . .

What kinds of things do you think about most frequently when you are by yourself? Make a private journal entry in which you record these thoughts.

Act 4, Scene 3

In this scene . . .

The scene takes place in Juliet's room. Juliet wishes to be left alone. She is now forced to take the potion a day early and doesn't know what the consequences of this action might be. Much of the scene is taken up with Juliet's fears about what the potion might do to her. However, trusting in the Friar, and considering the alternative of not consuming the potion, she swallows it, declaring, "Romeo, I come. This do I drink to thee."

1 *attires:* clothes

3 *orisons:* prayers

4 *my state:* the state of my soul

5 *cross:* perverse

7 *cull'd:* selected

8 *behoveful for our state:* befitting the splendour of the wedding

18 *What should . . . here?:* How could she help me?

23 *This:* a knife or dagger, worn at that time likely as part of daily dress, as much for ornament as for practical use

25 *Subtly hath minister'd:* has cleverly provided

Scene 3

Juliet's chamber.

Enter Juliet and Nurse.

Juliet: Ay, those attires are best; but, gentle nurse,
I pray thee, leave me to myself to-night;
For I have need of many orisons
To move the heavens to smile upon my state,
Which, well thou know'st, is cross and full of sin.   5
[Enter Lady Capulet.]
Lady Capulet: What, are you busy, ho? Need you my help?
Juliet: No, madam; we have cull'd such necessaries
As are behoveful for our state to-morrow.
So please you, let me now be left alone,
And let the nurse this night sit up with you;   10
For, I am sure, you have your hands full all,
In this so sudden business.
Lady Capulet: Good-night.
Get thee to bed, and rest; for thou hast need.
                    [Exeunt Lady Capulet and Nurse.]
Juliet: Farewell! God knows when we shall meet again.
I have a faint cold fear thrills through my veins,   15
That almost freezes up the heat of life.
I'll call them back again to comfort me.
Nurse!—What should she do here?
My dismal scene I needs must act alone.
Come, vial.   20
What if this mixture do not work at all?
Shall I be married then to-morrow morning?
No, no; this shall forbid it. Lie thou there.
                    [Laying down a dagger.]
What if it be a poison, which the friar
Subtly hath minister'd to have me dead,   25
Lest in this marriage he should be dishonour'd,
Because he married me before to Romeo?

29   *still been tried:* always been proved to be

32   *redeem:* rescue; *fearful point:* a horrible thought

37   *conceit:* idea, vision

42   *green in earth:* freshly buried

43   *festering:* rotting

47   *mandrakes':* The root of the mandrake, or mandragora, plant was thought to resemble the human shape and, when torn from the earth, to utter shrieks which drove those who heard them mad.

49   *distraught:* distracted, driven mad

50   *Environed . . . fears:* surrounded by all these frightening objects

51   *madly:* in my madness

52   *mangled:* He had been slain in a duel.

56   *spit:* pierce

I fear it is; and yet, methinks, it should not,
For he hath still been tried a holy man.
How if, when I am laid into the tomb,   30
I wake before the time that Romeo
Come to redeem me? There's a fearful point!
Shall I not then be stifled in the vault,
To whose foul mouth no healthsome air breathes in,
And there die strangled ere my Romeo comes?   35
Or, if I live, is it not very like,
The horrible conceit of death and night,
Together with the terror of the place,—
As in a vault, an ancient receptacle,
Where, for this many hundred years, the bones   40
Of all my buried ancestors are pack'd;
Where bloody Tybalt, yet but green in earth,
Lies festering in his shroud; where, as they say,
At some hours in the night spirits resort;—
Alack, alack, is it not like that I,   45
So early waking, what with loathsome smells,
And shrieks like mandrakes' torn out of the earth,
That living mortals, hearing them, run mad:
O, if I wake, shall I not be distraught,
Environed with all these hideous fears?   50
And madly play with my forefathers' joints?
And pluck the mangled Tybalt from his shroud?
And, in this rage, with some great kinsman's bone
As with a club, dash out my desperate brains?
O, look! methinks I see my cousin's ghost   55
Seeking out Romeo, that did spit his body
Upon a rapier's point. Stay, Tybalt, stay!
Romeo, I come! This do I drink to thee.
          [She falls upon her bed, within the curtains.]

Act 4, Scene 3: Activities

1. What do you think causes Juliet to picture the terrible images that she uses in her soliloquy (lines 14-58)? Make certain that your explanation uses evidence from the speech. Share your explanation with a partner and then revise it as necessary.

2. Rehearse Juliet's soliloquy, using the following guidelines:
   • Decide what Juliet is really saying.
   • Emphasize key words that are essential to meaning.
   • Create a mood that is appropriate to the situation.
   • Convey emotion by varying your voice.

   Present a reading to members of your group. Select the best reading from your group and present it to the entire class. You may wish to tape your reading and present it that way. Since women did not play parts in plays in Shakespeare's time, it might be interesting to hear a male reading of the soliloquy. Ask yourself, "Does a male reading change the impact of the speech in any way?"

3. If you were able to give Juliet some personal advice about her proposed actions, what would you say to her? Present your advice in one of the following ways:
   • as a speech from an imaginary character in the play
   • as a letter from an anonymous and concerned admirer in the play
   • as a journal entry beginning, "Juliet, if I could talk to you . . ."

For the next scene . . .

Have you ever hosted a very important party at your house? Describe the preparations you have had to make on the day of the party. What things did you worry about and what humorous incidents occurred?

Act 4, Scene 4

In this scene . . .

In this brief scene, preparations are being made for the wedding feast. Capulet supervises the proceedings, urging his servants to hurry so that everything will be ready on time. Capulet calls for the Nurse to awaken Juliet, for it is already early on the morning of the wedding day and Juliet needs to be properly attired for the festive occasion. Capulet announces that the bridegroom has already arrived and urges all the others to hasten.

2   *pastry:* the large bake-room where the paste for bread and "baked meats" (line 5) was made

4   *curfew-bell:* The bell ordinarily used for the curfew has on this special occasion been rung to arouse the house.

6   *cot-quean:* Literally, a cottage queen, a servant, but here applied humorously to Capulet, who is busying himself with so-called woman's work

8   *watching:* waiting up

9   *whit:* bit

11   *mouse-hunt:* woman chaser

12   *watch:* prevent

13   *a jealous-hood:* jealousy, a jealous woman

17   *drier logs:* for the pastry-room fire

21   *whoreson:* literally, a bastard, but here just a friendly manner of speech

22   *logger-head:* blockhead

24   *The County . . . straight:* A great wedding would be an all-day affair. Quite early the bride would be awakened and dressed by her attendants. (Here, for dramatic purposes, it is the Nurse who is sent to awaken Juliet.) Soon the bridegroom, accompanied by his attendants and musicians, would arrive to salute the bride with music. Thus the groom would "claim" his bride.

Scene 4

Hall in Capulet's house.

Enter Lady Capulet and Nurse.

Lady Capulet: Hold, take these keys, and fetch more spices, nurse.

Nurse: They call for dates and quinces in the pastry.
[Enter Capulet.]

Capulet: Come, stir, stir, stir! the second cock hath crow'd,
The curfew-bell hath rung, 'tis three o'clock.
Look at the baked meats, good Angelica;   5
Spare not for cost.

Nurse: Go, you cot-quean, go,
Get you to bed. Faith, you'll be sick to-morrow
For this night's watching.

Capulet: No, not a whit! What! I have watch'd ere now
All night for lesser cause, and ne'er been sick.   10

Lady Capulet: Ay, you have been a mouse-hunt in your time;
But I will watch you from such watching now.
     [Exeunt Lady Capulet and Nurse.]

Capulet: A jealous-hood, a jealous-hood!
*[Enter three or four Serving-men, with spits, logs, and
    baskets.]*
               Now, fellow,
What's there?

First Servant: Things for the cook, sir; but I know not what.   15

Capulet: Make haste, make haste.   *[Exit First Servant.]*
Sirrah, fetch drier logs;
Call Peter, he will show thee where they are.

Second Servant: I have a head, sir, that will find out logs.
And never trouble Peter for the matter.   20

Capulet: Mass, and well said; a merry whoreson, ha!
Thou shalt be logger-head.   *[Exit Second Servant.]*
Good faith, 'tis day.
The County will be here with music straight,

27   *trim her up:* adorn her; dress her appropriately

For so he said he would. I hear him near.   25
                                   [Music within.]
Nurse! Wife! What, ho! What, nurse, I say!
[Re-enter Nurse.]
Go waken Juliet, go and trim her up;
I'll go and chat with Paris. Hie, make haste,
Make haste; the bridegroom he is come already.
Make haste, I say.   *[Exeunt.]*   30

Act 4, Scene 4: Activities

1. Many people think this scene is silly because it doesn't add anything to the play. Discuss this opinion in groups and decide, as a director, what you would do with the scene in your production of *Romeo and Juliet*.

2. Choose an imaginary character, for example, a servant in the Capulet household. For a week, keep the journal that this character might write. Some suggestions for the character's journal are given below:
   - the things he or she would see
   - the conversations he or she would overhear or engage in
   - the kinds of duties he or she might perform
   - the kind of room he or she might live in
   - what the character thinks of his or her job
   - what the character thinks of his or her employers.

   You may find other areas that you could explore as well.

3. As a group activity, rewrite this short scene in modern dialogue and present it to the class.

For the next scene . . .

Frequently humour is developed around dull-witted characters who do not understand what is going on. Give an account of such a situation either from experience or from a television program or movie you have seen.

Act 4, Scene 5

In this scene . . .

The Nurse attempts to awaken Juliet but cannot. The potion has done its job. Finally, Juliet is declared to be dead, and Lady Capulet cries, "O woeful time!" Friar Laurence and the musicians enter to perform the wedding ceremony, along with Paris, only to find Capulet, Lady Capulet, and the Nurse mourning Juliet's untimely death. The Friar at this point reminds the gathered company that Juliet will find eternal peace in Heaven and reasons that mourning, therefore, is inappropriate. Capulet decides that the proposed wedding shall now give way to a funeral and that the preparations that he has spent all night making will shift their function from merriment to mourning. At the end of the scene, Peter and the musicians engage in some humorous banter about music. This appears rather tasteless, considering the solemnity of the events which have just occurred; however, it can be argued that they do not understand the implications of the events that have led up to the present situation.

2   *slug-a-bed:* slug in a bed, i.e., lazy one

6   *hath set up his rest:* is determined

15   *well a-day:* alas the day

16   *aqua vitae:* alcoholic spirits

18   *O heavy day!:* What a sorrowful day!

Scene 5

Juliet's chamber.

Enter Nurse.

Nurse: Mistress! what, mistress! Juliet!—Fast, I warrant
   her, she.—
Why, lamb! why, lady! fie, you slug-a-bed!
Why, love, I say, madam! sweetheart! why, bride!
What, not a word? you take your pennyworths now:
Sleep for a week; for the next night, I warrant,   5
The County Paris hath set up his rest
That you shall rest but little. God forgive me,
Marry, and amen, how sound is she asleep!
I needs must wake her. Madam, madam, madam!
Ay, let the County take you in your bed;   10
He'll fright you up, i'faith. Will it not be?
              [Undraws the curtains.]
What, dress'd, and in your clothes! and down again!
I must needs wake you. Lady! lady! lady!
Alas, alas! Help, help! my lady's dead!
O, well a-day, that ever I was born!   15
Some *aqua vitæ*, ho! My lord! my lady!
[Enter Lady Capulet.]
Lady Capulet: What noise is here?
Nurse: O lamentable day!
Lady Capulet: What is the matter?
Nurse: Look, look! O heavy day!
Lady Capulet: O me, O me! My child, my only life,
Revive, look up, or I will die with thee!   20
Help, help! Call help.
[Enter Capulet.]
Capulet: For shame, bring Juliet forth; her lord is come.
Nurse: She's dead, deceased, she's dead; alack the day!

26   *settled:* stopped or coagulated

37   *deflowered:* blighted

41   *thought long:* long anticipated

45   *In lasting . . . pilgrimage:* in his long and toilsome journey

48   *catch'd:* taken, snatched

55   *Beguiled:* tricked; *spited:* wronged

58   *not life . . . death!* He changes his mind; she is no longer his love in life, but his love in death.

Lady Capulet: Alack the day, she's dead, she's dead, she's
    dead!
Capulet: Ha! let me see her. Out, alas! she's cold;   25
    Her blood is settled, and her joints are stiff;
    Life and these lips have long been separated.
    Death lies on her like an untimely frost
    Upon the sweetest flower of all the field.
Nurse: O lamentable day!
Lady Capulet: O woeful time!   30
Capulet: Death, that hath ta'en her hence to make me wail,
    Ties up my tongue, and will not let me speak.
[Enter Friar Laurence and Paris, with Musicians.]
Friar Laurence: Come, is the bride ready to go to church?
Capulet: Ready to go, but never to return.
    O son! the night before thy wedding-day   35
    Hath Death lain with thy wife. See, there she lies,
    Flower as she was, deflowered by him.
    Death is my son-in-law, death is my heir;
    My daughter he hath wedded. I will die
    And leave him all; life, living, all is Death's.   40
Paris. Have I thought long to see this morning's face
    And doth it give me such a sight as this?
Lady Capulet: Accurst, unhappy, wretched, hateful day!
    Most miserable hour that e'er time saw
    In lasting labour of his pilgrimage!   45
    But one, poor one, one poor and loving child,
    But one thing to rejoice and solace in,
    And cruel Death hath catch'd it from my sight!
Nurse: O woe! O woeful, woeful, woeful day!
    Most lamentable day, most woeful day,   50
    That ever, ever, I did yet behold!
    O day! O day! O day! O hateful day!
    Never was seen so black a day as this.
    O woeful day, O woeful day!
Paris: Beguiled, divorced, wronged, spited, slain!   55
    Most detestable death, by thee beguiled,
    By cruel cruel thee quite overthrown!
    O love! O life! not life, but love in death!
Capulet: Despised, distressed, hated, martyr'd, kill'd!

61   *solemnity:* wedding festival

65-66   *Confusion's cure . . . confusions:* The cure for such ruin does not lie in such confused cries of grief.

71   *promotion:* advancement in this world by marriage

72   *your heaven:* your idea that heaven for you lay in this marriage

73   *advanced:* raised

77-78   *She's not . . . young:* The Friar is referring to the belief that it is good to die young when the soul is still pure.

79   *rosemary:* Rosemary, the flower of remembrance, was used at both weddings and funerals.

80   *corse:* corpse

83   *Yet nature's . . . merriment:* Yet reason laughs at our natural grief because the dead are happier than we are. We should be happy and not weep.

84   *ordained:* intended for our

85   *office:* proper use

94   *lour:* scowl, frown

Uncomfortable time, why camest thou now   60
To murder, murder our solemnity?
O child! O child! my soul, and not my child!
Dead art thou! Alack! my child is dead;
And with my child my joys are buried.
Friar Laurence: Peace, ho, for shame! Confusion's
    cure lives not   65
In these confusions. Heaven and yourself
Had part in this fair maid; now heaven hath all,
And all the better is it for the maid.
Your part in her you could not keep from death,
But heaven keeps his part in eternal life.   70
The most you sought was her promotion,
For 'twas your heaven she should be advanced;
And weep ye now, seeing she is advanced
Above the clouds, as high as heaven itself?
O, in this love, you love your child so ill,   75
That you run mad, seeing that she is well.
She's not well married that lives married long;
But she's best married that dies married young.
Dry up your tears, and stick your rosemary
On this fair corse; and, as the custom is,   80
In all her best array bear her to church;
For though fond nature bids us all lament,
Yet nature's tears are reason's merriment.
Capulet: All things that we ordained festival,
Turn from their office to black funeral;   85
Our instruments to melancholy bells,
Our wedding cheer to a sad burial feast,
Our solemn hymns to sullen dirges change,
Our bridal flowers serve for a buried corse,
And all things change them to the contrary.   90
Friar Laurence: Sir, go you in; and, madam, go with him:
And go, Sir Paris; every one prepare
To follow this fair corse unto her grave.
The heavens do lour upon you for some ill;
Move them no more by crossing their high will.   95
    [Exeunt Capulet, Lady Capulet, Paris, and Friar.]
First Musician: Faith, we may put up our pipes, and be
    gone.

101   *Heart's ease:* a popular song of the time

105   *dump:* sad song. The "merry" is Peter's idea of a joke.

112   *gleek:* jest

112-113 *I will . . . minstrel:* I will call you minstrel, probably because a minstrel was a "gleeman" or "gleekman."

114   *give you the serving-creature:* reply by calling you mere servant

116   *I will . . . crotchets:* I will endure none of your whims. There is also a pun on "crotchets" in its musical meaning of "quick time." *I'll re . . . fa you:* I'll play a tune on your head with my stick. "Re" and "fa" are notes in the musical scale.

117   *Do you note me?:* Do you understand (or heed) me? (extends the pun on musical notes)

121   *Then have . . . wit!:* Then here is an attack with my wit!

128-33 *Catling . . . Rebeck . . . Soundpost:* Catling derived his name from a small lute-string made of catgut; Rebeck's name is that of a three-stringed instrument played with a bow, mentioned by many writers; and Soundpost's name refers to the wooden peg fixed below the bridge of the stringed instrument.

132   *sound for silver:* play for money

133   *Pretty too!:* Not bad!

Nurse: Honest good fellows, ah, put up, put up;
   For, well you know, this is a pitiful case.   *[Exit.]*
First Musician: Ay, by my troth, the case may be amended. 100
   [Enter Peter.]
Peter: Musicians, O, musicians, "Heart's ease, Heart's ease!"
   O, an you will have me live, play "Heart's ease."
First Musician: Why "Heart's ease"?
Peter: O, musicians, because my heart itself plays "My heart
   is full of woe." O, play me some merry dump to comfort 105
   me.
First Musician: Not a dump we; 'tis no time to play now.
Peter: You will not, then?
First Musician: No.
Peter: I will then give it you soundly.   110
First Musician: What will you give us?
Peter: No money, on my faith, but the gleek; I will give
   you the minstrel.
First Musician: Then will I give you the serving-creature.
Peter: Then will I lay the serving-creature's dagger on your 115
   pate. I will carry no crotchets; I'll *re* you, I'll *fa* you.
   Do you note me?
First Musician: An you *re* us and *fa* us, you note us.
Second Musician: Pray you, put up your dagger, and put
   out your wit.   120
Peter: Then have at you with my wit! I will dry-beat you
   with an iron wit, and put up my iron dagger.
   Answer me like men:
      "When griping grief the heart doth wound,
      And doleful dumps the mind oppress,   125
      Then music with her silver sound"—
   why "silver sound"? Why "music with her silver sound"?
   What say you, Simon Catling?
First Musician: Marry, sir, because silver hath a sweet sound.
Peter: Pretty! What say you, Hugh Rebeck?   130
Second Musician: I say "silver sound," because musicians
   sound for silver.
Peter: Pretty too! What say you, James Soundpost?
Third Musician: Faith, I know not what to say.
Peter: O, I cry you mercy; you are the singer. I will say 135

139   *redress:* comfort

141   *Jack:* scoundrel; tarry; wait for

142   *stay dinner:* stay to dinner

for you. It is "music with her silver sound," because
musicians have no gold for sounding:
   "Then music with her silver sound
   With speedy help doth lend redress."   *[Exit.]*
First Musician: What a pestilent knave is this same!   140
Second Musician: Hang him, Jack! Come, we'll in here, tarry
   for the mourners, and stay dinner.   *[Exeunt.]*

Act 4, Scene 5: Activities

1. Based on previous evidence and on previous decisions that you have reached, do you believe that Capulet is sincere when he says, "And with my child my joys are buried?" What do you think makes him say such a thing? Why did it take him so long to realize how much his daughter meant to him?

2. In groups, discuss whether Capulet has behaved as a typical father. What would you say to Capulet? Put your response in the form of a letter. Remember to use evidence to support your reasoning. Also remember to use the proper tone in your letter. Capulet is a nobleman. If you prepared your letter on a word processor, would you send it to Capulet in that form? Why or why not?

3. In groups, discuss the following problem:
   When Friar Laurence speaks about death and eternal life, many people believe that he is not twisting the truth but, rather, is stepping outside himself and telling the audience his deepest beliefs. He can now make the Capulets accept truths about themselves that they couldn't accept before. If you accept that the Friar is telling his beliefs, what new truths does he convey to the Capulets? If you don't accept this, then what *is* Friar Laurence trying to do? Report your ideas to the class.

4. Capulet's parting words in this scene are "And all things change them to the contrary." To what extent do you believe that this statement is a description of the action of the play so far? Discuss this with your group and make a point-form outline that you can use later as the basis for an essay. Put your outline in your writing folder.

5. A burlesque is a form of comedy that uses exaggeration to ridicule a serious subject or situation. In groups, decide in what way the scene between Peter and the Musicians is burlesque. Keep a record of your discussion for

further research into the burlesque. Are there any modern forms of burlesque writing? If you were presenting the play to a modern audience, would you cut this part of the scene or leave it in?

6. Reread the journal entries you made for your imaginary character in the Activities for Act 4, Scene 4, page 242. Write about how he or she would have reacted to the news of Juliet's death. Share this writing with others in the class.

Act 4: Consider the Whole Act

1. Giving your own reactions, write a paper completing two or three of the following statements:
   - I believe that Juliet has/has not changed significantly since the beginning of the play because . . .
   - Friar Laurence's plan for Juliet is/is not likely to succeed because . . .
   - I would/would not consider doing what Juliet decides to do because . . .
   - When Juliet was discovered "dead," I felt . . . because . . .
   - What I find most difficult to understand in this act is . . .
   - What I have discovered so far about Juliet is . . .

2. Many people feel that the part of Act 4 dealing with Peter and the Musicians has no place in the play. Would you cut this part of the scene because it detracts from the sombre mood, or would you leave it in because it lightens the sombre mood? Discuss your opinion with your group.

3. Friar Laurence's advice to Juliet might be summed up in his comment, "be strong and prosperous in this resolve" (Act 4, Scene 1, lines 122-23). If you could put yourself in the play at this point, what would you say to Juliet and the Friar? Would either of them listen to you?

4. If Juliet had the opportunity to write a letter to Romeo at the end of Scene 1, what would she say? What would be the general tone of her letter? Since she no longer trusts the Nurse, how would she have the letter delivered to Romeo?

5. Each member of your group could select a short, emotional speech by a major character in this act. Then you could write the line numbers of your selected speech on a piece of paper, fold the paper, and place it in a central container. Each member would then draw one piece of paper. The person who draws a piece of paper would pantomime the emotion of the speech by using only body movements and facial expressions. When the group recognizes the emotion, the person pantomiming has succeeded. This should be a timed activity.

6. Select a figure of speech (simile, metaphor, personification, oxymoron) that you found to be particularly effective in this act. List as many associations as you can think of that apply to the figure of speech. Write an explanation of your figure of speech. Explain how it fits into the scene. Present your findings to your group.

7. Props are important in a play because they add dramatic interest and help to establish setting. Elizabethan theatre used very few props, yet still managed to capture the imagination of the audience. Act out the sequence at the beginning of Scene 2 where the servants prepare for Juliet's wedding. Turn your classroom into a stage. Some of the class will be major actors, and the rest will be the minor actors. Make props that you think will be appropriate. Remember to choreograph your scene carefully so that your props work the way you want them to.

8. *Make a video*
This activity is best done in pairs or in small groups. Select a part of a scene in this act in which you focus on the tension between two characters. You have forty-five sec-

onds of TV time to get your message across to your audience. Good luck!

Consider the following as you prepare your shooting script:
- You must catch the viewers' attention immediately.
- Make your point early in the sequence.
- Don't bore the audience with unnecessary dialogue – they want action. This means you may have to cut and edit dialogue.

For the next scene . . .

Most movie and television heroes we admire are the ones who finally decide to fight against whatever odds confront them. Who is your favourite hero or heroine? What is it that you admire about him or her the most?

Act 5, Scene 1

In this scene . . .

Balthasar brings Romeo the news of Juliet's death. Romeo challenges Fate to change its present course and then decides to go to Juliet's tomb, regardless of the possible consequences of such an action. Despite Balthasar's advice, Romeo decides to "lie" with Juliet that very night. To that end, he seeks an apothecary who will sell him a "dram of poison." He finds the individual and makes the purchase.

1   *the flattering truth:* what bears the flattering semblance of truth

2   *presage:* foretell, predict

3   *bosom's lord:* heart

10   *possess'd:* when actually enjoyed

11   *but love's shadows:* the dreams of love; Scene Direction: *booted:* still wearing his riding boots, to suggest his haste

18   *Capels:* The Capulets

21   *took post:* rode hard

23   *for my office:* as my duty

24   *stars:* fate. Here, Romeo challenges Fate, which has caused him so much ill. He now defies Fate to alter his course.

28-29   *import some misadventure:* suggest some misfortune that will occur

Act 5, Scene 1

Mantua. A street.

Enter Romeo.

Romeo: If I may trust the flattering truth of sleep,
My dreams presage some joyful news at hand.
My bosom's lord sits lightly in his throne,
And all this day an unaccustom'd spirit
Lifts me above the ground with cheerful thoughts.   5
I dreamt my lady came and found me dead—
Strange dream, that gives a dead man leave to think!—
And breathed such life with kisses in my lips,
That I revived, and was an emperor.
Ah me! how sweet is love itself possess'd,   10
When but love's shadows are so rich in joy!
[Enter Balthasar, booted.]
News from Verona!—How now, Balthasar!
Dost thou not bring me letters from the friar?
How doth my lady? Is my father well?
How fares my Juliet? that I ask again;   15
For nothing can be ill, if she be well.
Balthasar: Then she is well, and nothing can be ill.
Her body sleeps in Capels' monument,
And her immortal part with angels lives.
I saw her laid low in her kindred's vault,   20
And presently took post to tell it you.
O, pardon me for bringing these ill news,
Since you did leave it for my office, sir.
Romeo: Is it even so? Then I defy you, stars!
Thou know'st my lodging; get me ink and paper,   25
And hire post-horses; I will hence to-night.
Balthasar: I do beseech you, sir, have patience.
Your looks are pale and wild, and do import
Some misadventure.

34   *lie with:* sleep with, Romeo will sleep with Juliet in death, and so the two will be lovers.

38   *late I noted:* recently I saw

40   *Culling of simples:* sorting over herbs; *meagre:* sparse, thin

42   *needy:* poorly furnished

43   *An alligator stuff'd:* This and the other items mentioned were regular parts of an apothecary's shop in Shakespeare's time.

45   *beggarly account:* scant supply

46   *bladders:* used for storing liquids

47   *packthread:* a tough thread used for sewing packs; *old . . . roses:* dried rose leaves pressed together, used as perfume

48   *make up a show:* to impress customers

49   *penury:* poverty

51   *sale . . . death:* the selling of which means death to the seller; i.e., it is a crime

52   *caitiff wretch:* miserable creature

59   *Hold:* here; *ducats:* coins varying in value but worth about two dollars in terms of our money, called ducats because they were issued by a duke

60   *gear:* matter

63   *trunk:* body

64   *hasty:* quick to explode

Romeo: Tush, thou art deceived:
Leave me, and do the thing I bid thee do.   30
Hast thou no letters to me from the friar?
Balthasar: No, my good lord.
Romeo: No matter; get thee gone
And hire those horses; I'll be with thee straight.
                              [Exit Balthasar.]
Well, Juliet, I will lie with thee to-night.
Let's see for means. O mischief, thou art swift   35
To enter in the thoughts of desperate men!
I do remember an apothecary,
And hereabouts he dwells, which late I noted
In tatter'd weeds, with overwhelming brows,
Culling of simples; meagre were his looks,   40
Sharp misery had worn him to the bones.
And in his needy shop a tortoise hung,
An alligator stuff'd, and other skins
Of ill-shaped fishes; and about his shelves
A beggarly account of empty boxes,   45
Green earthen pots, bladders and musty seeds,
Remnants of packthread and old cakes of roses,
Were thinly scatter'd, to make up a show.
Noting this penury, to myself I said,
"An if a man did need a poison now,   50
Whose sale is present death in Mantua,
Here lives a caitiff wretch would sell it him."
O, this same thought did but forerun my need,
And this same needy man must sell it me.
As I remember, this should be the house.   55
Being holiday, the beggar's shop is shut.
What, ho! apothecary!
[Enter Apothecary.]
Apothecary: Who calls so loud?
Romeo: Come hither, man. I see that thou art poor.
Hold, there is forty ducats. Let me have
A dram of poison, such soon-speeding gear   60
As will disperse itself through all the veins
That the life-weary taker may fall dead,
And that the trunk may be discharged of breath
As violently as hasty powder fired

66   *mortal:* fatal, deadly

67   *utters them:* passes them from one person to another

68   *bare:* stripped of dignity

70   *starveth . . . eyes:* can be seen in the look in your eyes, which tells me you are starving

71   *Contempt . . . back:* Your tattered clothes reveal that you are a beggar and held in contempt.

75   *My . . . consents:* My poverty makes me agree to do this, not my desire.

85   *cordial:* a drink that comforts and revives because it stimulates the heart

Doth hurry from the fatal cannon's womb.   65
Apothecary: Such mortal drugs I have; but Mantua's law
    Is death to any he that utters them.
Romeo: Art thou so bare and full of wretchedness,
    And fear'st to die? Famine is in thy cheeks,
    Need and oppression starveth in thine eyes,   70
    Contempt and beggary hangs upon thy back;
    The world is not thy friend nor the world's law;
    The world affords no law to make thee rich;
    Then be not poor, but break it, and take this.
Apothecary: My poverty, but not my will, consents.   75
Romeo: I pay thy poverty, and not thy will.
Apothecary: Put this in any liquid thing you will,
    And drink it off; and, if you had the strength
    Of twenty men, it would dispatch you straight.
Romeo: There is thy gold, worse poison to men's souls,   80
    Doing more murder in this loathsome world,
    Than these poor compounds that thou mayst not sell.
    I sell thee poison; thou hast sold me none.
    Farewell! Buy food, and get thyself in flesh.
    Come, cordial and not poison, go with me   85
    To Juliet's grave; for there must I use thee.

                               [Exeunt.]

Act 5, Scene 1: Activities

1. With a partner, read Romeo's first speech in this scene and discuss the premonition that he has. Decide whether Romeo should have altered his course of action. In your journal, write about a premonition you have had and the results of the premonition. Share your account.

2. In your journal, explain Romeo's actions after Balthasar tells him of Juliet's "death." Write your own personal reaction to Romeo's behaviour.

3. Romeo's detailed memory of the apothecary shop gives us some insight into what these shops looked like in ancient times. You might want to do further research in the library into what could be found in an apothecary's shop. Then you could compare and contrast your findings with what is on the shelves of a modern pharmacy. Perhaps you have friends whose relatives are pharmacists and who could give you more vivid descriptions.

4. What feelings do you think Romeo is experiencing as he describes his memory of the apothecary shop he visited? Decide whether this portion of the scene could be eliminated without damaging the play. Share your decision in a class discussion.

For the next scene . . .

List in your journal your group's decisions about the following questions:
- To what extent do you believe that fate determines what happens in the lives of all of us?
- Do you believe that the actions of others can sometimes determine what happens to you?
- How can the unexpected alter what a person may wish to do at any given time?

Act 5, Scene 2

In this scene . . .

Friar Laurence's plans go awry. Father John is unable to go to Mantua with the message for Romeo. Because he supposedly came in contact with a carrier of the plague, he is prevented from leaving the city of Verona. Friar Laurence's reaction is mixed: he feels fortune has gone against him, but he has a possible solution. He decides to go to the tomb of Juliet himself in order to awaken her, spirit her away, and keep her with him at his cell until Romeo can come to the cell himself. The two can then be united and escape.

4   *his mind be writ:* he has written down what he is thinking

6   *associate:* accompany. Franciscan friars usually had to travel
        in pairs.

8   *searchers:* officials responsible for the town's health

9   *house:* religious house

10   *infectious pestilence:* the Black Death (bubonic plague, which
        swept through Europe in the fourteenth and fifteenth centuries)

11   *Seal'd up the doors:* prevented anyone from entering or leaving.
        During the plague, houses were sealed up to ensure that the
        occupants did not go out and spread the disease.

12   *speed:* hasty journey; *stay'd:* prevented

17   *brotherhood:* the religious order to which he belonged

18   *nice:* a trifling matter; *charge:* important matters

19   *dear import:* serious concern; *neglecting it:* failure to deliver it

21   *crow:* crowbar; *straight:* right away

26   *beshrew:* blame

27   *accidents:* occurrences

Scene 2

Verona. Friar Laurence's cell.

Enter Friar John.

Friar John: Holy Franciscan friar! brother, ho!
[Enter Friar Laurence.]
Friar Laurence: This same should be the voice of Friar John.
   Welcome from Mantua! What says Romeo?
   Or, if his mind be writ, give me his letter.
Friar John: Going to find a bare-foot brother out,   5
   One of our order, to associate me,
   Here in this city visiting the sick,
   And finding him, the searchers of the town,
   Suspecting that we both were in a house
   Where the infectious pestilence did reign,   10
   Seal'd up the doors, and would not let us forth;
   So that my speed to Mantua there was stay'd.
Friar Laurence: Who bare my letter, then, to Romeo?
Friar John: I could not send it,—here it is again,—
   Nor get a messenger to bring it thee,   15
   So fearful were they of infection.
Friar Laurence: Unhappy fortune! By my brotherhood,
   The letter was not nice but full of charge
   Of dear import, and the neglecting it
   May do much danger. Friar John, go hence;   20
   Get me an iron crow, and bring it straight
   Unto my cell.
Friar John: Brother, I'll go and bring it thee.   *[Exit.]*
Friar Laurence: Now must I to the monument alone;
   Within this three hours will fair Juliet wake.   25
   She will beshrew me much that Romeo
   Hath had no notice of these accidents;
   But I will write again to Mantua,
   And keep her at my cell till Romeo come;
   Poor living corse, closed in a dead man's tomb!   *[Exit.]* 30

Act 5, Scene 2: Activities

1. Brainstorm with a partner and consider the following problem: If you were Friar Laurence and couldn't deliver your letter of instructions to Romeo, what alternative courses of action could you take? Make a list of possibilities. Which possibility would you use?

2. With a partner, reread the Prologue to the play. Make a list of any similarities that you find between the Prologue and this scene. What do you believe is the purpose of establishing this link?

3. The Prologue refers to Romeo and Juliet as being "star-cross'd." How does the outbreak of the plague in this scene affect the "star-crossed" lovers? Write a journal entry to yourself in which you assess whether or not anyone's life can be "star-cross'd."

For the next scene . . .

In a story or a movie, the ending is always the logical outcome of the situations and themes established at the beginning. It can usually be predicted fairly accurately. Before reading Scene 3, discuss in groups what you think the outcome of the following elements of the play will be. Record your predictions in your journal. Check them against what actually happens in Scene 3.
- the Montague-Capulet feud
- the deception carried out by both Romeo and Juliet
- the meddling of both the Nurse and Friar Laurence
- the idea that the two lovers are "star-cross'd"
- the determination of Paris to marry Juliet
- the fact that Romeo and Juliet believe everything they hear from adults and from friends
- the notion that, for Romeo and Juliet, love is somehow worth dying for.

Act 5, Scene 3

In this scene . . .

This scene occurs in the churchyard in Verona at night. Here Romeo, accompanied by Balthasar, comes to place flowers on Juliet's grave. Unknown to Romeo, Paris has arrived at exactly the same time to perform the same ritual. Romeo bids Balthasar to stay at a distance. He wants to be alone with Juliet in his grief. Balthasar, however, hides close by because he is afraid of what Romeo may intend to do. Romeo opens the tomb just as Paris approaches. Paris recognizes Romeo as a Montague and, fearing the worst, challenges him. When Romeo slays Paris, Paris asks to be placed with his betrothed, Juliet, in her tomb. Romeo complies with Paris's wishes and places him inside the tomb. Romeo asks forgiveness, declares his love again, drinks the poison, and dies. Friar Laurence discovers Romeo's body. Juliet awakens from her drugged sleep, discovers Romeo dead, takes up Romeo's dagger, and kills herself. The Watch alerts the town to the tragedy in the tomb. The Prince and the Capulets arrive first to discover the horror. Montague arrives later to announce the death of his wife over the exile of Romeo. The Prince hears Friar Laurence's explanation of the events leading up to the multiple deaths, receives from Balthasar the letter written by Romeo to his father, and makes his pronouncement on the entire proceedings of the play.

1   *stand aloof:* keep your distance

3   *all along:* at full length

13   *canopy:* covering over a four-poster bed

14   *sweet water:* perfumed water

15   *distill'd by moans:* created by my grief

16   *obsequies:* funeral rites and ceremonies; *keep:* observe

20   *cross:* interfere with

21   *Muffle:* conceal

22   *mattock:* an agricultural tool used for digging and chopping, shaped like a pick-axe with a wide end; *wrenching iron:* pry-bar

Scene 3

A churchyard; in it a tomb
belonging to the Capulets.

Enter Paris, and his Page, bearing
flowers and a torch.

Paris: Give me thy torch, boy. Hence, and stand aloof.
  Yet put it out, for I would not be seen.
  Under yond yew-trees lay thee all along,
  Holding thine ear close to the hollow ground;
  So shall no foot upon the churchyard tread,   5
  Being loose, unfirm, with digging up of graves,
  But thou shalt hear it. Whistle then to me,
  As signal that thou hear'st something approach.
  Give me those flowers. Do as I bid thee, go.
Page: [Aside.] I am almost afraid to stand alone   10
  Here in the churchyard; yet I will adventure.
                                            [Retires.]
Paris: Sweet flower, with flowers thy bridal bed I strew,—
  O woe! thy canopy is dust and stones—
  Which with sweet water nightly I will dew,
  Or, wanting that, with tears distill'd by moans.   15
  The obsequies that I for thee will keep
  Nightly shall be to strew thy grave and weep.
                                      [The Page whistles.]
  The boy gives warning something doth approach.
  What cursed foot wanders this way to-night,
  To cross my obsequies and true love's rite?   20
  What, with a torch! Muffle me, night, a while.
                                            [Retires.]
[Enter Romeo and Balthasar, with a torch, mattock, etc.]
Romeo: Give me that mattock and the wrenching iron.
  Hold, take this letter; early in the morning
  See thou deliver it to my lord and father.
  Give me the light. Upon thy life, I charge thee,   25

32   *dear:* important

33   *jealous:* suspicious

36   *hungry:* that is, for more corpses

37   *time:* night

38   *inexorable:* relentless, merciless

39   *empty:* hungry

41   *Take thou that:* Romeo hands him some money.

43   *For . . . same:* just the same

45   *maw:* stomach of a beast of prey; here, the tomb

48   *in despite:* out of hate for you; *more food:* that is, his own body
      shall further feed the "maw" (literally, stomach) of death

Whate'er thou hear'st or seest, stand all aloof,
And do not interrupt me in my course.
Why I descend into this bed of death,
Is partly to behold my lady's face;
But chiefly to take thence from her dead finger   30
A precious ring, a ring that I must use
In dear employment; therefore hence, be gone.
But if thou, jealous, dost return to pry
In what I further shall intend to do,
By heaven, I will tear thee joint by joint   35
And strew this hungry churchyard with thy limbs.
The time and my intents are savage-wild,
More fierce and more inexorable far
Than empty tigers or the roaring sea.
Balthasar: I will be gone, sir, and not trouble you.   40
Romeo: So shalt thou show me friendship. Take thou that;
    Live, and be prosperous; and farewell, good fellow.
Balthasar: *[Aside.]* For all this same, I'll hide me hereabout;
    His looks I fear, and his intents I doubt.   *[Retires.]*
Romeo: Thou detestable maw, thou womb of death,   45
    Gorged with the dearest morsel of the earth,
    Thus I enforce thy rotten jaws to open,
    And, in despite, I'll cram thee with more food!
                                    [Opens the tomb.]
Paris: This is that banish'd haughty Montague,
    That murder'd my love's cousin, with which grief,   50
    It is supposed, the fair creature died;
    And here is come to do some villainous shame
    To the dead bodies. I will apprehend him.
                                    [Comes forward.]
    Stop thy unhallow'd toil, vile Montague!
    Can vengeance be pursued further than death?   55
    Condemned villain, I do apprehend thee.
    Obey, and go with me; for thou must die.
Romeo: I must indeed, and therefore came I hither.
    Good gentle youth, tempt not a desperate man.
    Fly hence, and leave me; think upon these gone,   60
    Let them affright thee. I beseech thee, youth,
    Put not another sin upon my head,
    By urging me to fury: O, be gone!

68   *conjurations:* serious appeals or pleas

74   *peruse:* look closely at

76   *betossed:* deeply agitated

77   *attend:* pay heed to

78   *should have:* was to have

82   *One . . . book!:* One, like me, entered in the list of the unfortunate!

84   *lantern:* turret full of windows to admit light

86   *feasting presence:* a state room suitable, because of its light, for feasts held by kings

87   *a dead man:* a man shortly to be dead, i.e., himself

90   *A lightning before death:* a lightening of the soul that occurs before death; also, a flash of illumination that occurs before death

94-6   *Thou art . . . there:* As long as beauty's red flag is seen in Juliet's cheeks and lips, the white flag of death cannot be raised.

By heaven, I love thee, better than myself;
For I come hither arm'd against myself.   65
Stay not, be gone; live, and hereafter say
A madman's mercy bade thee run away.
Paris: I do defy thy conjurations,
And apprehend thee for a felon here.
Romeo: Wilt thou provoke me? Then have at thee, boy!   70
[They fight.]
Page: O Lord, they fight! I will go call the watch.
[Exit.]
Paris: O, I am slain! *[Falls.]* If thou be merciful,
Open the tomb, lay me with Juliet.   *[Dies.]*
Romeo: In faith, I will. Let me peruse this face.
Mercutio's kinsman, noble County Paris!   75
What said my man, when my betossed soul
Did not attend him as we rode? I think
He told me Paris should have married Juliet.
Said he not so? Or did I dream it so?
Or am I mad, hearing him talk of Juliet,   80
To think it was so? O, give me thy hand,
One writ with me in sour misfortune's book!
I'll bury thee in a triumphant grave.
A grave? O, no! a lantern, slaughter'd youth,
For here lies Juliet, and her beauty makes   85
This vault a feasting presence full of light.
Death, lie thou there, by a dead man interr'd.
[Laying Paris in the tomb.]
How oft when men are at the point of death
Have they been merry! which their keepers call
A lightning before death. O, how may I   90
Call this a lightning? O my love! my wife!
Death, that hath suck'd the honey of thy breath,
Hath had no power yet upon thy beauty.
Thou art not conquer'd; beauty's ensign yet
Is crimson in thy lips and in thy cheeks,   95
And death's pale flag is not advanced there.
Tybalt, liest thou there in thy bloody sheet?
O, what more favour can I do to thee,
Than with that hand that cut thy youth in twain
To sunder his that was thine enemy?   100

103   *unsubstantial:* without material shape, i.e., without body

105   *paramour:* mistress

106   *still:* always

110   *Will I . . . rest:* I will remain here forever. "To set up one's rest" was a gambling phrase, "the rest" being the highest stake the parties wished to risk.

111   *yoke . . . stars:* the burden of an adverse fate

115   *dateless:* for eternity; *engrossing Death:* Death will finally win everything.

116   *conduct:* conductor

118   *rocks:* that is, of death; *bark:* that is, ship of life

121   *be my speed!:* help me (to reach the tomb quickly)

122   *stumbled:* to stumble was regarded as a bad omen

124   *Bliss . . . you!:* May God bless you.

Forgive me, cousin! Ah, dear Juliet,
Why art thou yet so fair? Shall I believe
That unsubstantial death is amorous,
And that the lean abhorred monster keeps
Thee here in dark to be his paramour? 105
For fear of that, I still will stay with thee,
And never from this palace of dim night
Depart again. Here, here will I remain
With worms that are thy chamber-maids; O, here
Will I set up my everlasting rest, 110
And shake the yoke of inauspicious stars
From this world-wearied flesh. Eyes, look your last!
Arms, take your last embrace! and, lips, O you
The doors of breath, seal with a righteous kiss
A dateless bargain to engrossing Death! 115
Come, bitter conduct, come, unsavoury guide!
Thou desperate pilot, now at once run on
The dashing rocks thy sea-sick weary bark!
Here's to my love! *[Drinks.]* O true apothecary!
Thy drugs are quick. Thus with a kiss I die. *[Dies.]* 120
[Enter at the other end of the churchyard, Friar Laurence,
with a lantern, crow, and spade.]
Friar Laurence: Saint Francis be my speed! how oft to-night
Have my old feet stumbled at graves! Who's there?
Balthasar: Here's one, a friend, and one that knows you
well.
Friar Laurence: Bliss be upon you! Tell me, good my friend,
What torch is yond, that vainly lends his light 125
To grubs and eyeless skulls? As I discern,
It burneth in the Capels' monument.
Balthasar: It doth so, holy sir; and there's my master,
One that you love.
Friar Laurence: Who is it?
Balthasar: Romeo.
Friar Laurence: How long hath he been there?
Balthasar: Full half an hour. 130
Friar Laurence: Go with me to the vault,
Balthasar: I dare not, sir.
My master knows not but I am gone hence;
And fearfully did menace me with death

136   *ill:* evil

142   *masterless:* without masters or owners

143   *discolour'd:* stained with blood

148   *comfortable:* full of comfort

152   *contagion:* poison

155   *in thy bosom:* lying there in your arms

162   *timeless:* untimely

163   *churl:* unmannerly person (an endearing reproach)

164   *help me after:* help me follow you

165   *Haply:* perhaps

166   *a restorative:* a healing medicine

If I did stay to look on his intents.
Friar Laurence: Stay, then; I'll go alone. Fear comes upon
    me: 135
O, much I fear some ill unlucky thing.
Balthasar: As I did sleep under this yew-tree here,
    I dreamt my master and another fought,
    And that my master slew him.
Friar Laurence: Romeo!   *[Advances.]*
Alack, alack, what blood is this, which stains   140
The stony entrance of this sepulchre?
What mean these masterless and gory swords
To lie discolour'd by this place of peace?
                      [Enters the tomb.]
Romeo! O, pale! Who else? What, Paris too?
And steep'd in blood? Ah, what an unkind hour   145
Is guilty of this lamentable chance!
The lady stirs.   *[Juliet rises.]*
Juliet: O comfortable friar! where is my lord?
    I do remember well where I should be,
    And there I am. Where is my Romeo?   150
                  [Noise within.]
Friar Laurence: I hear some noise. Lady, come from that
    nest
Of death, contagion, and unnatural sleep.
A greater power than we can contradict
Hath thwarted our intents. Come, come away.
Thy husband in thy bosom there lies dead;   155
And Paris too. Come, I'll dispose of thee
Among a sisterhood of holy nuns.
Stay not to question, for the watch is coming;
Come, go, good Juliet, I dare no longer stay.
Juliet: Go, get thee hence, for I will not away.   160
           [Exit Friar Laurence.]
What's here? A cup, closed in my true love's hand?
Poison, I see, hath been his timeless end.
O churl! drunk all, and left no friendly drop
To help me after? I will kiss thy lips;
Haply some poison yet doth hang on them,   165
To make me die with a restorative.   *[Kisses him.]*
Thy lips are warm.

169   *happy:* Juliet will be happy to use the dagger.

173   *attach:* arrest

179-80 *ground . . . ground:* in the first instance "ground" is used to mean "earth," but in the second instance it means "cause"

181   *circumstance:* all the facts

188   *What . . . up:* What tragedy has occurred so early in the morning?

190   *should:* can

194   *startles:* causes alarm

First Watch: [Within.] Lead, boy; which way?
Juliet: Yea, noise? Then I'll be brief. O happy
    dagger!   *[Snatching Romeo's dagger.]*
  This is thy sheath *[Stabs herself]*; there rust, and
    let me die.   *[Falls on Romeo's body, and dies.]*   170
  [Enter Watch, with the Page of Paris.]
  Page: This is the place; there, where the torch doth burn.
First Watch: The ground is bloody; search about the
    churchyard.
  Go, some of you, whoe'er you find attach.
  Pitiful sight! here lies the County slain;
  And Juliet bleeding, warm, and newly dead,   175
  Who here hath lain this two days buried.
  Go, tell the Prince; run to the Capulets;
  Raise up the Montagues; some others search.
  We see the ground whereon these woes do lie;
  But the true ground of all these piteous woes   180
  We cannot without circumstance descry.
  [Re-enter some of the Watch, with Balthasar.]
Second Watch: Here's Romeo's man; we found him in the
    churchyard.
First Watch: Hold him in safety till the Prince come hither.
  [Re-enter Friar Laurence, and another Watchman.]
Third Watch: Here is a friar, that trembles, sighs, and weeps.
  We took this mattock and this spade from him,   185
  As he was coming from this churchyard side.
First Watch: A great suspicion. Stay the friar too.
  [Enter the Prince and Attendants.]
Prince: What misadventure is so early up,
  That calls our person from our morning rest?
  [Enter Capulet, Lady Capulet, and others.]
Capulet: What should it be, that they so shriek abroad?   190
Lady Capulet: The people in the street cry Romeo,
  Some Juliet, and some Paris; and all run,
  With open outcry, toward our monument.
Prince: What fear is this which startles in our ears?
First Watch: Sovereign, here lies the County Paris slain;   195
  And Romeo dead; and Juliet, dead before,
  Warm and new kill'd.
Prince: Search, seek, and know how this foul murder comes.

203 *mista'en:* mistaken its proper place; *house:* scabbard or sheath

206 *bell:* passing or funeral bell

214-15 *what manners . . . grave?:* It is not mannerly for the young to precede their elders – a pathetic remark in this context.

216 *Seal . . . outrage:* Cease this outrageous talk.

217 *ambiguities:* unexplained happenings

219 *general . . . woes:* director of your grievances

220 *even to death:* even though it means the death penalty for offenders

221 *let mischance . . . patience:* Let misfortune be endured patiently.

222 *parties of suspicion:* suspected persons

223-5 *I am the greatest . . . murder:* Although I was least able because of my age and physical condition to commit this crime, yet because of circumstances, I am most open to suspicion.

226 *impeach:* accuse; *purge:* clear

229 *my short . . . breath:* the short time I have left to live

233 *stolen:* secret

237 *siege:* pressure

First Watch: Here is a friar, and slaughter'd Romeo's man,
    With instruments upon them, fit to open   200
    These dead men's tombs.
Capulet: O heavens! O wife, look how our daughter bleeds!
    This dagger hath mista'en,—for, lo, his house
    Is empty on the back of Montague,—
    And is mis-sheathed in my daughter's bosom!   205
Lady Capulet: O me! this sight of death is as a bell,
    That warns my old age to a sepulchre.
    [Enter Montague and others.]
Prince: Come, Montague; for thou art early up,
    To see thy son and heir more early down.
Montague: Alas, my liege, my wife is dead to-night;   210
    Grief of my son's exile hath stopp'd her breath.
    What further woe conspires against mine age?
Prince: Look, and thou shalt see.
Montague: O thou untaught! what manners is in this,
    To press before thy father to the grave?   215
Prince: Seal up the mouth of outrage for a while,
    Till we can clear these ambiguities,
    And know their spring, their head, their true descent;
    And then will I be general of your woes,
    And lead you even to death. Meantime forbear,   220
    And let mischance be slave to patience.
    Bring forth the parties of suspicion.
Friar Laurence: I am the greatest, able to do least,
    Yet most suspected, as the time and place
    Doth make against me, of this direful murder;   225
    And here I stand, both to impeach and purge
    Myself condemned and myself excused.
Prince: Then say at once what thou dost know in this.
Friar Laurence: I will be brief, for my short date of breath
    Is not so long as is a tedious tale.   230
    Romeo, there dead, was husband to that Juliet;
    And she, there dead, that Romeo's faithful wife.
    I married them; and their stolen marriage-day
    Was Tybalt's dooms-day, whose untimely death
    Banish'd the new-made bridegroom from this city,   235
    For whom, and not for Tybalt, Juliet pined.
    You, to remove that siege of grief from her,

243   *tutor'd:* taught

247   *as this:* on this

255   *closely:* in secret

266   *is privy:* shares the secret

270   *still:* always

273   *in post:* in great haste

Betroth'd and would have married her perforce
To County Paris. Then comes she to me,
And, with wild looks, bid me devise some mean   240
To rid her from this second marriage,
Or in my cell there would she kill herself.
Then gave I her, so tutor'd by my art,
A sleeping potion; which so took effect
As I intended, for it wrought on her   245
The form of death. Meantime I writ to Romeo,
That he should hither come as this dire night,
To help to take her from her borrow'd grave,
Being the time the potion's force should cease.
But he which bore my letter, Friar John,   250
Was stay'd by accident, and yesternight
Return'd my letter back. Then all alone
At the prefixed hour of her waking,
Came I to take her from her kindred's vault;
Meaning to keep her closely at my cell,   255
Till I conveniently could send to Romeo;
But when I came, some minute ere the time
Of her awaking, here untimely lay
The noble Paris and true Romeo dead.
She wakes; and I entreated her come forth,   260
And bear this work of heaven with patience.
But then a noise did scare me from the tomb;
And she, too desperate, would not go with me,
But, as it seems, did violence on herself.
All this I know; and to the marriage   265
Her nurse is privy; and, if aught in this
Miscarried by my fault, let my old life
Be sacrificed, some hour before his time,
Unto the rigour of severest law.
Prince: We still have known thee for a holy man.   270
Where's Romeo's man? What can he say to this?
Balthasar: I brought my master news of Juliet's death;
And then in post he came from Mantua
To this same place, to this same monument,
This letter he early bid me give his father,   275
And threaten'd me with death, going in the vault,
If I departed not and left him there.

280   *made your master:* was your master doing

292   *scourge:* dreadful punishment

293   *That heaven . . . love!:* that heaven has used the love of Romeo and Juliet to destroy your happiness

294   *winking at:* closing my eyes to

295   *brace of kinsmen:* Mercutio and Paris

297   *jointure:* marriage dower

301   *at such rate:* of such high value

305   *glooming:* gloomy

Prince: Give me the letter; I will look on it.
   Where is the County's page, that raised the watch?
   Sirrah, what made your master in this place?   280
Page: He came with flowers to strew his lady's grave;
   And bid me stand aloof, and so I did.
   Anon comes one with light to ope the tomb,
   And by and by my master drew on him;
   And then I ran away to call the watch.   285
Prince: This letter doth make good the friar's words,
   Their course of love, the tidings of her death.
   And here he writes that he did buy a poison
   Of a poor 'pothecary, and therewithal
   Came to this vault to die, and lie with Juliet.   290
   Where be these enemies? Capulet! Montague!
   See, what a scourge is laid upon your hate,
   That heaven finds means to kill your joys with love!
   And I, for winking at your discords too,
   Have lost a brace of kinsmen. All are punish'd.   295
Capulet: O brother Montague, give me thy hand.
   This is my daughter's jointure, for no more
   Can I demand.
                 But I can give thee more;
Montague: For I will raise her statue in pure gold;
   That whiles Verona by that name is known,   300
   There shall no figure at such rate be set
   As that of true and faithful Juliet.
Capulet: As rich shall Romeo's by his lady's lie,
   Poor sacrifices of our enmity!
Prince: A glooming peace this morning with it brings;   305
   The sun, for sorrow, will not show his head.
   Go hence to have more talk of these sad things;
   Some shall be pardon'd, and some punished:
   For never was a story of more woe
   Than this of Juliet and her Romeo.   *[Exeunt.]* 310

Act 5, Scene 3: Activities

1. Most everyone has experienced a graveyard at night. Recall an experience of your own, telling a partner what you saw, how you felt, and what thoughts you had at the time. Record your experience in your journal. Explain how your experience helped you to understand the mood of this scene.

2. With a partner, note all the unexpected events that occur in this scene. Decide how these are linked with the idea that fate shapes the events of the play. Share your ideas with the whole class.

3. Imagine that fate is an actual character. Consider the following:
   - What would Fate look like?
   - How would Fate act?
   - How would Fate dress?
   - What would Fate say to somebody if it chose to speak?

   Read your description to members of your group. Agree on a general description and have an artist draw a picture of your vision of Fate. What position might Fate play on a hockey team?

4. Modern directors often find that the last part of the scene featuring the Prince is too long for modern audiences. How would you shorten it and still keep the tone that Shakespeare intended?

5. What, if anything, has the older generation learned at the end of the play about itself and about the relationship that should have existed between itself and the younger generation? Discuss this problem in groups. Share your findings with the rest of the class.

6. Who are the people in the play who contributed in some way to the deaths of Romeo and Juliet? Make a list of

them and show how they were involved. Write your opinions of the actions of each person. Put one of these characters on trial. In groups of four, have one half of the group prepare the prosecution side of a court argument. The other half will prepare the defence side. Have the members of another group act as a jury. Present the two arguments, and note the verdict reached by the jury.

7. Write an obituary column for either Romeo or Juliet (or both) as it might appear in a prominent newspaper or news magazine.

8. Write a journal entry in which you express your reactions to the play as a whole.

Consider the Whole Play

1. Review the actions of Romeo and Juliet in the play and record how they attempted to deal with their problems. List the problems that Juliet faced on one side of a page and note the actions she took to deal with them on the other side. Do the same with Romeo. Could either one have changed the course of events by acting differently? Why do you think so? Share your responses with others in your group or class.

2. Write a political commentary of the play as it might appear in your favourite newspaper or your favourite magazine. You might include topics such as:
   • the breakdown of the family
   • violence in society
   • laws that don't work
   • weapons controls
   • the role of religion in politics.

3. Write a children's story using the characters and the main events in this play.
   a) Decide the age or grade level for whom the story

will be written. If possible, select a junior or senior elementary school student who will be your reader, and consult this student as you begin your plans for the story. Find out, for example, what type of story this student likes to read and, also, what kinds of pictures he or she thinks are important for a book. (They might be cut out of old magazines.) Perhaps you could arrange to interview your young student reader so that he/she becomes a part of your project.

b) Discuss the kind of ending your story should have with your reader.

c) Remember to use simple vocabulary and sentence structure suitable for the grade level you have chosen.

d) Present your story to your reader's group or class.

Have the children evaluate your story so you can determine its success.

4. In pairs, prepare a two-minute tape of a conversation between Romeo and Juliet that is *not* in the text but that emphasizes a central theme. Play the tape to the class. You can determine your success by seeing if the class can locate a place where your taped conversation could fit into the action of the play.

5. Soap operas are a favourite form of contemporary entertainment. How could *Romeo and Juliet* be made into a "soap"? Create a rough outline of how it might be done.

6. Write a soliloquy in modern English focussing on some aspect of a main character's self-deception. You might choose one of the following:
   • Romeo's delusions about love
   • Tybalt's argument for revenge
   • Mercutio's ideas about manhood
   • Friar Laurence's ideas about virtue.

Share your soliloquy with the class.

7. Throughout the play, Romeo and Juliet's romance has been linked to death, beginning in Act 1, Scene 5, lines 119-20. With a partner, make a list of the ten most memorable references. With your partner, consider whether or not there is a connection between these references and Friar Laurence's reference to Juliet as a "living corse" at the end of Act 5, Scene 2. Share these findings with your group and with the class as a whole. You might find the Prologue useful in your research.

8. There are many fights throughout the play, including the final one between Romeo and Paris. With a partner, make a list of all the fights in the play, determine what causes each fight, list the fighters, and decide what effect each fight has on the development of the play. Write a paper about the effects the fighting has on the lives of Romeo and Juliet. Write a journal entry in which you record your thoughts about the effects of fighting on the lives of people in general.

9. Examine newspaper and magazine articles on teenage suicide. What advice would you give to teenagers who consider suicide? What advice would you give to Romeo and Juliet? Write a private journal entry recording your own thoughts about this subject.

10. A potion is a dose of medicine that either cures or poisons. Research some of the common potions used in Elizabethan England to cure illnesses. Make a list of these potions and see how many of them are used today. When you are undertaking your research, consider the question, "Why would a Friar be interested in potions?" Knowing what you do about potions, what advice might you give the Friar at this time? Make a journal entry describing your feelings about taking drugs in general.

11. There are many stories about famous lovers in Greek and Roman mythology. Prepare a list of these stories and videos with the help of the librarian. Make brief plot outlines of your stories, and prepare brief character

sketches noting the similarities you have found between them and Romeo and Juliet. Discuss this project with your teacher to make sure that you are on the right track. Keep all your notes and rough drafts in a separate folder. Prepare a written, an oral, or a visual summary of your findings and conclusions at the end of the time period specified for your independent activity. Decide why these stories have remained so popular to readers, viewers, and writers to the present day.

12. Prepare a documentary on the lives of Romeo and Juliet in which you concentrate on the question, "Who was really responsible for their deaths?" Keep in mind that a documentary
    • uses informed comments to help people better understand the events that have happened
    • poses a question to be answered
    • obtains as many points of view as possible
    • gives a full background to the situation
    • allows the viewers or listeners the freedom to make up their own minds.

Present your audio- or videotaped documentary to the class.

13. You are a director. Select a self-contained part of a scene that you particularly like. Then do the following:
    • Decide what the main idea is.
    • Decide how to express that idea.
    • Emphasize characters and character relationships.
    • Plan exits and entrances.
    • Make a sketch of the set so you can plan the action.

Create a "prompt" book in which you use marginal notes to show script cuts, stage directions, indications for pauses, phrasing, and emphasis in difficult passages, sketches or diagrams showing actors' positions, and cues for lights and other effects.

Working with a group, direct your part of the scene, using the prompt sheets you have prepared. Present the scene to the class.

14. Prepare a slide-show documentary of the main events of *Romeo and Juliet.* Use members of your class to stage the incidents you believe to be the key ones in each act. Photograph each of these incidents on slides. Write a monologue to connect the incidents. Choose appropriate background music for your slides so that the whole presentation makes an emotional and visual impact. Make sure that each member of your group has an opportunity to contribute something to the production. The following might help:
    - Make sure that the narrative does not overstate the content of the slides themselves.
    - Make sure that the music is appropriate.
    - Make sure that your production does not "drag."
    - Make sure that the slides flow smoothly from one to the next.
    - Keep your production within a fifteen-minute time frame.

15. Prepare a portion of a scene for a video production. Select a part of a scene that reveals something specific about the emotional state of a character and videotape it without using dialogue. Consider the following before you make your video:
    - Who will be the audience for your video production?
    - What emotion do you wish to focus on?
    - How will you achieve the effect of the emotion?

    Prepare a video script. Be sure to observe the following:
    - Use effective camera angles.
    - Use distance effectively.
    - Balance your shots.
    - Use colour and lighting to create different effects.

    Remember to decide on the number and order of the shots you will use *before* you shoot. Add appropriate music to your video and show the completed segment to the class.